Ameri~~~
Cooking
in England

*American cooking ingredients,
measurements, and recipes
translated to British English*

Delora Jones

GLENCOE HOUSE PUBLICATIONS
BURTON UPON TRENT

Author's note:
Although the title of this book is *American Cooking in England*, many of its entries apply to other parts of the British Isles as well. I used 'England' in the title rather than 'Britain' because that is where I live and that is the market I know (and the one the book is based on). Scotland, Wales, and Ireland have their own foods and markets and titling the book 'in Britain' would have ignored this fact. However, I have pointed out regional or national differences in food names or preparations whenever I've been aware of them.

Cover photograph by Lynn Silverman; all other photographs by Delora Jones. Cover design by Visual Communication, Burton upon Trent.

First published 1998 by Glencoe House Publications
PO Box 5149, Burton upon Trent, Staffordshire DE14 3WZ

British Library Cataloguing in Publication Data
A catalogue record for this book is available from the British Library.

ISBN 0-9533557-0-5

Printed in Great Britain by John Mackie, Burton upon Trent

This book is dedicated
to the memory of my mother

MILDRED RUTH JONES

ACKNOWLEDGEMENTS

There were a great number of books and organisations I looked to for answers to my many questions and I cannot list them all, but I will list those who were especially helpful: *British Sugar, Boots Pharmaceuticals*; *Common Ground,* London; *Birdseye Walls*; *Staffordshire Trading Standards*; *Poly-Lina Ltd.*; *Tate & Lyle Sugars*; *the Flour Advisory Bureau*; *the National Association of Cider Makers*; *BRLA*; *the National Dairy Council (UK); the National Dairy Council (US); MAFF (Ministry of Agriculture, Fisheries, and Food)*; *British Meat*; *Nestlé*; *the British Egg Information Service*; *British Trout Association*; *the Sea Fish Industry Authority*; *Home-Grown Cereals Authority*; *Supercook* (Baking powder); *Azko Nobel Salt, Inc.; Westmill Foods Ltd.*; and the staff at *Burton Library.*

I also wish to thank all those people who provided recipes, offered editorial advice, or who helped out in other ways: Mildred and Edgar R. Jones; Delora Griffin; Mid Sarchioto; Leah Ryel; Jean Ranallo; Ed Jones; Gladys Jones and Anita Montanile; Jan and Al Smith; Cindy Hoyle; Gail Harris; Bea Dunn; Lynne Wilson; Neisha Bassoff; Rhiannon Williams; Louise and Clare Owen; and especially to my friends and relatives who helped proofread and/or test recipes: Michele Barber; Lynn Silverman and John Penny; Steve Bayliss; John Hadamuscin; and also Roz Denny (who virtually proofread the book when I sent it to her to review -- many thanks indeed).

When the book was completed, I was faced with the daunting task of publishing it myself. I've managed to do this, thanks to some long-distance help from Anne Mavor of Portland, Oregon, who'd published her own book two years ago, and pointed me in the right directions (and there are many).

A very special thanks are due my husband, Roger Owen. If it were not for his support and encouragement, you would not be reading this book.

TABLE OF CONTENTS

INTRODUCTION

When I first moved from the US to England, my trips to the supermarket which should have taken 20 minutes often stretched to 45. Where's the tomato sauce? What's single cream? Is double-concentrated tomato puree the same as tomato paste? Where's the corn syrup? Are there *any* sodas without artificial sweeteners? Things were stocked differently, packaged differently, and called differently, and the issue was muddied by the fact that the American and English language sometimes call different things by the same name (e.g., biscuit, cider).

Necessity is the mother of invention and that's how this book came to be. I needed a guide to tell me what I was looking for, where to find it, and whether or not it's even available here, but that guide didn't exist. Now, thanks to 5 years of work and research, it does.

American Cooking in England is designed not just for Americans living in England but also for anyone who owns a cookbook written for the American market (it could be Chinese even, but if it calls for a half-cup of snow peas, it's written in American).

This book is comprised of 5 sections:

Food Names: In this, the main part of the book, I've translated the names of food items from American to English, and provided instructions on where to find these foods (or suitable substitutes). Also included are individual beef, lamb, pork and veal sections that tell you which cut to use when a particular American cut is called for, and how to cook it; plus diagrams of the American and British cuts.

Measurements: I've included here the charts which proved most helpful to me in cooking, such as quick reference charts for dry and fluid measures; milk and cream charts showing equivalent fat contents; American cup, package, and can size conversions; etc.

Recipes: This section does not purport to represent a cross-section of American recipes, merely a cross-section of the recipes I found useful living here in England, including recipes for substitutes; recipes for dishes they don't make here (or make differently than in the US, like lasagne); and recipes I had trouble finding (like *Rice Krispies Treats*).

Useful Information: I've kept this section short to prevent it spiralling out into its own book. This section simply explains a few things that caused me confusion when first I arrived here, like switches on electrical outlets (*electrical points*); the difference between a tied pub and a freehouse; etc. -- it's not just a common language that divides our two cultures.

Plus, a *Mail Order and Shopping Guide.*

There is also a pocketbook that complements this main book (see page 240). The pocketbook is designed to fit easily into a pocket or handbag for quick access when grocery shopping (or to keep by the cooker for quick measurements conversions, especially for things like 'a half-stick of butter'). It contains an abridged version of the aforementioned *Food Names* section, and a *Measurements* section.

American Cooking in England was written during the 1990s and reflects the two languages (and cuisines) of this time; the same book written in the 1960s would be completely different. Language and cuisine are subject to all sorts of influences (such as waves of immigration), and the changes wrought by these influences often reflect an area's history. Lately, however, it seems the main influence on language has been through television; when I tuned in the other night, 3 out of England's 5 'terrestrial' channels were airing American programmes. I do not wish to see English become Americanised as a result of television; these sorts of changes to language do not inform us about an area's history, they are simply a side-effect of technology. My intention in writing *American Cooking in England* was to provide a key to understanding the differences between American and English that cause especial confusion in the kitchen. And, frustrating though this may be to recently-arrived Americans ("What do you *mean* there are no serviettes!?"), I wish to see our two languages and cultures remain distinct. One of these days I might even learn English.

Burton upon Trent, September 1998   Delora Jones

FOOD NAMES

This section of the book is essentially an A-Z of American foods, ingredients, and related items. The American name appears on the left and the English translation (or rough equivalent) appears in italics on the right. For any American ingredients which are either not available here or are difficult to locate, I have tried to give instructions for suitable substitutes. If you know the English name but not the American name, then check the Index.

Almonds, sliced	*Flaked almonds*
Anchovy paste	*Anchovy essence*
Angel hair pasta	*Vermicelli*

Angel hair pasta is a very fine spaghetti formed into pasta nests. It is sometimes available in British supermarkets and goes by a variety of names, including *vermicelli*. Angel hair pasta is a wheat-based vermicelli, not to be confused with the Oriental rice-based vermicelli.

Appetizer	*Starter*

Apple butter — Fruit butters are purees made from fruit, sugar and spices. Butter is not an ingredient, it is simply a word meaning a puree that's thicker than a jam but not as thick as a paste. As of this writing, apple butter is not sold in English supermarkets but you can get it from some farms. To make your own, see the recipe on page 193.

Apple jack — Apple jack is apple brandy made from fermented apple cider.

Apples, candied	*Toffee apples*
Apples, McIntosh	*Empire apples*, a cross between McIntosh and Delicious, are a reasonable substitute for Macs and are available in many supermarkets (usually imported from the US). McIntosh are not normally grown in the UK as they are prone to canker.
Arugula	*Rocket* or *roquette* The herb arugula or *rocket* is a dark green leaf with a spicy, almost hot flavour -- a bit intense on its own. *Rocket* is widely used in Italian cuisine and is good in salads, sandwiches, and cream cheese. Many supermarkets carry it, either fresh or in seed packets. If you can't find it fresh, you can easily grow it from seeds.
Bacon	*Rindless unsmoked streaky bacon* also called *Danish plain (or unsmoked) streaky rindless bacon* *Streaky* bacon and American bacon come from the same section of the pig, though American bacon is usually cut a bit thinner than *streaky*,[1] yields more fat, and is saltier. (See also the Bacon entry on page 87 in the Pork Cuts section.) To cook *streaky* bacon for use in BLTs,[2] do the following:

- Heat a large, heavy-bottomed skillet until hot. Add 1 teaspoon oil and heat the oil until it's runny. Turn the pan to coat the bottom of it with the hot oil.

---

[1]American bacon is about 1/16" thick.

[2]A BLT is a bacon, lettuce, and tomato sandwich.

- Reduce the heat to low and add one layer of the *streaky bacon.*
- Turn the bacon as it cooks, pressing down the fatty areas so they become crispy.
- Once the bacon is lightly browned, put it on paper towels (*kitchen paper*) to drain.

Bacon rashers are slices of bacon.

Bacon, Canadian

Canadian-style bacon is made from the loin muscle of the pig which is rolled and cured and then sold in large pieces or in slices. It is more like ham than bacon in both taste and appearance, and is suitable for roasting, broiling (*grilling*), and frying. In Canada, it is called back bacon. A *gammon steak* would make a reasonable substitute. (For the differences between *gammon* and ham, see the introduction to the Pork Cuts section on page 79.)

Bag, garbage

Bin liner

Bag, plastic grocery

Carrier or *carrier bag*
When the check-out person asks if you'd like a carrier, she's asking if you need a bag to put your groceries in. The term *carrier* (meaning a plastic bag) is unknown in the US.

Bagels

Some supermarkets carry packaged bagels but fresh bagels can be difficult to find (unless you live near a Jewish quarter). To make your own bagels , see the recipe on page 156.

Baking powder

American baking powder is double-acting, that is, it contains two acidulants -- a fast one that reacts in cold dough and a slow-acting one that reacts to warmth. British baking powder is single-acting, containing just the slow acidulant. When using British baking powder in American recipes, *do not* double the amount. I recommend leaving the measurement 'as is' and only adjusting it if you find it necessary. (I have not had to adjust the amounts in the American recipes I've used.)

Baking soda

Bicarbonate of soda
In England, *bicarbonate of soda* is usually sold in small round plastic containers and not in large cardboard boxes as it is in the US.

Barley

Pearl barley

L-R: British baking powder, American baking powder and baking soda, and British bicarbonate of soda (i.e., baking soda).

Beans, bush	*Dwarf beans*
Beans, fava	*Broad beans*
Beans, French-cut	Beans sliced lengthwise into thin strips are known in the US as 'Frenched' or 'French-cut' beans.
Beans, garbanzo	*Chick peas*
Beans, lima	*Butter beans* In recipes calling for lima beans, you may substitute using *butter beans*. Lima beans originated in Peru (hence their name) and are sold fresh, canned, and frozen in the US. Canned lima beans are soft, flat, mildly sweet, and with a smooth rather than a pasty consistency; frozen lima beans tend to be plump and firm, with a pasty consistency -- more like the English canned butter beans.
Beans, navy	*Haricot beans* Navy beans, pea beans, and Boston beans are all names for *haricot beans*. These are the beans used for making Boston baked beans.
Beans, pole	*Climbing beans* or *runner beans*
Beans, string or green or snap	*Round beans*, *French beans* or *green beans* *Round beans* are the same as American string beans; *French beans* are immature green beans and as such, are a bit thinner than the typical American green bean. *Runner beans* may be used if the others are unavailable but if they've got a string, you'll want to remove that first. In the US, green, snap, and wax beans all used to be called 'string beans' but most modern

varieties are now stringless; nonetheless, the
name 'string bean' for the most part hangs on.

Beans, yellow wax

Yellow wax beans are like a yellow French
bean and, as of this writing, their seeds are not
available in England (although they have been
available in the past). If you want wax beans,
you'll need to bring the seeds back with you
from America.

Beef cuts

See following page.

Beef jerky

Beef jerky and *biltong*
Jerky (from the Spanish, *charqui*) can mean
plain, unseasoned dried meat; seasoned and
dried meat strips; or smoked and cured meat
strips. In America, beef jerky is eaten as a
snack and is a common back-packing food.
Biltong is a South African word meaning strips
of sun-dried meat. Whereas beef jerky is often
seasoned with smoke essence or a garlic
seasoning, biltong is commonly seasoned with
coriander. Beef jerky is difficult to find in
England but is available from Partridges and
Harrods, and both beef jerky and biltong are
available from Susmans (see *Mail Order &
Shopping Guide* section).

BEEF CUTS

American cuts of beef and British cuts of beef do not always have exact counterparts. The method I use to reduce guesswork when shopping for beef in England is to see what section of the cow the meat is from, then see what that part of the cow is called in England. If there's still a question, I ask the butcher.

I have listed below some popular American cuts of beef. Their descriptions usually include the American name of the section of cow the cut is from and, if the British name of the same (or roughly the same) section of cow is different, I've included that in italics.

Châteaubriand	The steaks used for making Châteaubriand are cut on the diagonal from the thickest part of the tenderloin or *fillet of beef* and range in thickness from 2" - 3" (*5-7.5cm*). Châteaubriand is broiled (*grilled*) and served with a béarnaise sauce.
Chuck cross rib, chuck rib, chuck roast, chuck arm steak	'Chuck' cuts come from the chuck or chuck shoulder section of the cow. The same section in England is called *chuck* or *chuck blade*. In Scotland, *chuck* and *blade* combined are known as *shoulder*.
Club steak	*See Top loin steak.*
Corned beef brisket	The meat used for making corned beef (*salt beef*) is cut from the breast portion of the brisket, near the front leg, and is flat and boneless. The name corned beef comes from Anglo Saxon times when the granular salt used to process it was the size of a kernel of wheat (*corn*).

BEEF CUTS, *cont.*

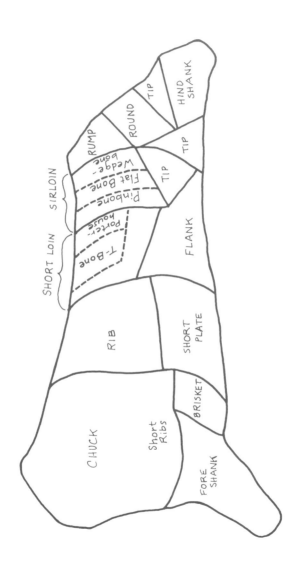

AMERICAN BEEF CUTS

BEEF CUTS, *cont.*

BRITISH BEEF CUTS

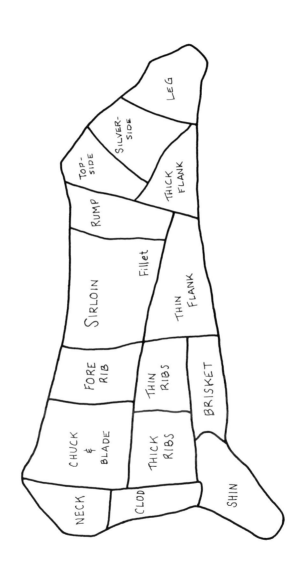

BEEF CUTS, *cont.*

Cubed steak   *Stewing steak*

Delmonico steak   *Rib eye steak*
                       These 1" (*2.5cm*) boneless steaks are cut from
                       the eye of the rib roast and in the US, are also
                       known as Spencer steaks and rib eye steaks.

Eye of Rib roast   The eye of the rib roast is the boned-out centre
                       of the rib roast with the less tender meat
                       removed. As the name implies, eye of rib roasts
                       come from the eye of the rib (*forerib*) section,
                       and are tied into roasts which normally produce
                       around 24 slices. This is the roast from which
                       Delmonico or Spencer steaks (*rib eye steaks*)
                       are cut and, in England, is the traditional cut of
                       roast beef.

Filet mignon   *Filet mignon* or *filet mignon tournedos*
                       These small fillet steaks are cut from the end or
                       near the tip of the tenderloin or *fillet of beef*,
                       and are usually sliced fairly thin, pounded, and
                       flattened.

Fillet steaks   These cuts go by the same name in England as
                       in the US. Fillet steaks are cut from
                       approximately the centre of the tenderloin or
                       fillet of beef and range in thickness from
                       1½" - 2" (*4-5cm*).

Foreshank   *Shin*
                       In England, the foreshank section of the cow is
                       called the *shin*.

BEEF CUTS, *cont.*

Ground beef

Minced beef
Minced beef is made from less tender cuts of meat and is sold in a fine or coarse mince; the fine mince is similar to American ground beef. In the US, ground beef is made from cuts such as chuck, flank, brisket, and round; in England, it's more likely to come from sections such as *thin flank, neck & clod, and thin rib*.

Hindshank

Leg
In England, the hindshank section of the cow is called the *leg*.

Loin tenderloin steak   *Fillet steak*

London broil or flank steak

London broil is an inexpensive and boneless cut of meat from the flank section, i.e., the belly area below the loin. Although it is also known as flank steak in the US, it is not related to British flank.

Porterhouse steak

In the US, Porterhouse steak comes from the part of the cow called the short loin; in England, this same part of the cow is from their *sirloin* section. The Porterhouse has a larger portion of the tenderloin and a longer tail than the T-bone steak.

Rib eye steaks

See Delmonico steak.

Rib roast or prime rib

Most rib or rib eye roasts and steaks come from the rib (*forerib*). The cross rib pot roast, however, is from the chuck section.

BEEF CUTS, *cont.*

Round steak or
round roast

This is the same cut of meat as is used for the English cut called *rump steak* and is taken from the top of the hindquarter. 'Round' cuts are from the round section which roughly encompasses the *silverside, topside* and *thick flank* sections of British beef.

Sandwich steak

To make sandwich steak, use *very* thinly sliced steak from the round section (in England, from either the *topside* or *silverside* sections). Sandwich steak is made by frying the thinly sliced meat in some fat, usually with sautéed onions.

Shank

The foreshank is the *shin*; the hindshank is the *leg*.

Shell steak

See Top loin steak.

Short plate

In the US, this section of the cow lies between the flank and brisket so in England, it lies at the *brisket* end of the *flank* or *thin flank* section.

Short ribs and
chuck short ribs

Short ribs are cut from the ribs between the rib section and the short plate section of the cow; chuck short ribs are cut from the ribs between the chuck section and the brisket section. Roasts for home use are often cut short and the resulting cut-off rib ends are the short ribs which are normally braised or marinated and barbecued.

BEEF CUTS, *cont.*

Sirloin steak	Sirloin steak comes from the hip bone section of the sirloin and is leaner than (but not as tender as) the Porterhouse and T-bone steaks from the adjoining short loin section. In England, the sirloin and short loin sections are considered one section, called *sirloin*. These steaks contain different shapes and sizes of marrowbone and go by the following names: pinbone (nearest the Porterhouse), flat-bone, round-bone, and wedge-bone sirloin steaks.
Sirloin steak, boneless	*Entrecôte* *Entrecôte* is a boneless steak which consists of the eye of the loin meat from the *sirloin* (but not including the fillet). *Entrecôte steaks* are usually cut 1-1½" thick *(2.5-4cm)*.
Spencer steak	*See Delmonico steak.*
Swiss steak	Swiss steak is made from a 1½" *(4 cm)* thick cut of meat from the rump, round, or chuck sections of the cow (called *rump, topside, silverside,* or *chuck and blade* sections in England). To make Swiss steak, tenderise the meat with a meat pounder or hammer, coat it with seasoned flour (flour/salt/ pepper) and brown it in a little fat in a frying pan.
T-bone steak	In the US, this cut comes from the part of the cow called the short loin; in England, this same

BEEF CUTS, *cont.*

part of the cow is from their *sirloin* section.
The American T-bone has a smaller portion of
the tenderloin and a shorter tail than the
Porterhouse steak.

Tenderloin of beef   *Fillet of beef*
or fillet of beef
The tenderloin or *fillet of beef* is the choicest,
most tender cut of beef. In the US, it comes
from the section of the cow called the short-
loin; in England, it's found tucked underneath
the bone of the same section (called in England
sirloin). From the tenderloin come such cuts as
fillet steaks, tournedos, filet mignons and the
cut for making Châteaubriand. The tenderloin
is used whole in dishes such as Beef
Wellington.

Tenderloin steak   *Fillet steak*

Top loin steaks
When the top loin section of the cow is boned
out, the fillet removed, and the remaining meat
then cut into steaks, the result is top loin steaks.
Examples of top loin steaks include strip steak,
shell steak, club steak, New York cut, Kansas
City cut, etc.

Tournedos
These 1" (*2.5cm*) steaks go by the same name in
England as in the US and are cut from near the
centre of the tenderloin or *fillet of beef.*

Beer	*Lager* In the US, the term 'beer' covers pretty much all types of beer but in general, when an American asks for a beer, they mean a *lager*. In England, you ask for a specific type of beer (e.g., *mild*, *lager*, *stout*); if you just ask for *beer* you'll get *bitter*, the well-hopped and often darker-coloured English beer (not to be confused with Angostura bitter*s*, also alcoholic). Beer is readily available in supermarkets, off-licenses, and pubs. (See Beer and Pubs in *Useful Information* section.)
Beets	*Beetroot*
Biscuit	*Scone* (not a sweet scone) American rolled biscuits are essentially the same as oven scones. Both American biscuits and oven scones are made from flour; shortening; baking powder and/or soda; and milk. To make your own biscuits, see the recipe on page 161.
Biscuit cutter	*Pastry cutter*
Blueberries	Fresh blueberries are very difficult to locate in England. In his book *Food Watch*, Drew Smith said they are usually available from July to September but as of this writing, I've only seen them once -- in Stafford in January! However, if you live near Dorset or Wolverhampton, you can pick your own (around August to September) at James Trehane & Sons or Essington Fruit Farm. (For addresses, see the *Mail Order and Shopping Guide* section.) Blueberries are small, smooth, round, blueish-

black berries commonly used in the US for making jam, pancakes, muffins, pies and other baked goods, or as a topping for cheesecakes, but best of all on their own (or with a little cream). They are a member of the bilberry family but are larger, juicier and less tart than the British bilberry.

Bluefish	Bluefish is a soft textured fish with loose, moist flakes and is moderately oily. The relatively dark flesh cooks to a light off-white colour. There is no exact substitute in Britain.
Bologna	*Polony* *Polony* may come from either Polonia (medieval Latin term for Poland) or Bologna, Italy. It is often available at deli counters in British supermarkets. *Polony* normally has a smaller diameter than the typical US bologna and is usually cut more thickly.
Boston baked beans	Boston baked beans originated as a Puritan dish and are made of navy (*haricot*) beans which are slowly baked in a rich dark sauce for 6-9 hours.
Bouillon cubes	*Stock cubes* (e.g., Kallo's 'Just Bouillon') or *stock granules*
Bread	In England, bread refers to the same thing as it does in the US. However, zucchini bread, banana bread, pumpkin bread and any sweet bread would, in England, be called *cakes*.
Bread, Italian	Italian bread sold in America is like a soft-crusted French stick, but shorter (around a foot

long [*30 cm*]) and about three times as thick. It is often decorated with sesame seeds.

Bread rolls   *Baps* or *plain tea cakes* or *cobs*.

Broad noodles or wide noodles   Broad or wide noodles are the noodles used in making noodle kugel (noodle pudding). They measure approximately $^7/_{16}$" wide (*11mm*) as opposed to around $^3/_{16}$" (*5mm*) for a regular flat noodle width. Wide noodles are difficult to find in England, other than in speciality shops.

Broccoli   *Broccoli* or *calabrese.*

Broil   *Grill*
In England, the verb *broil* was in common use during Victorian times. Since then, it has been replaced with the word *grill* but has not been replaced in the US. 'Broil' is normally used in the US to refer to food cooked in a broiler (*grill*, UK) while 'grill' is normally used in the US to refer to food cooked on a barbecue. See 'broiler', below.

Broiler   *Grill*
In English *cookers* (stoves, US), the broiler is called the *grill* and is usually situated either above the main oven in a compartment which sometimes doubles as a second oven, or else above the *hob* (stovetop, US), at about eye-level. Broilers in American electric stoves are often combined with the main oven while in American gas stoves, they're usually in a separate compartment beneath the main oven.

Broiler (chicken)	*Spring chicken* A *spring chicken* (broiler, US) weighs about 2½ pounds.
Broth, chicken	Canned chicken broth is available in some speciality food shops but is not normally available in the supermarket -- most people either make their own broth or make do with stock cubes. To make your own broth, see page 212 of the Recipes section.
Brownies	Brownies are a moist, chewy, flat cake, usually around 1" (*2.5cm*) high and baked in a rectangular or square pan. The most common brownies are chocolate and contain walnuts. For a recipe, see page 179.
Buns, sweet	*Tea cakes*
Burner	A gas burner is called a gas burner while an electric burner is called a *ring*; you would say 'turn off the *ring*' rather than 'turn off the burner' if it's an electric *cooker*.
Burritos	Burritos, a Mexican dish which has gained popularity in the US, are made with flour (rather than corn) tortillas that are wrapped around a bean and/or meat filling and warmed in the oven.
Butter, drawn	*Clarified butter*
Butter, sweet	*Unsalted butter*
Butter, whipped	Use *spreadable butter* (e.g., Lurpak, Anchor)
Butterfly shrimp	*Prawn cutlet*

Buttermilk	Originally, buttermilk was the liquid runoff remaining after cream had been soured and churned into butter. Modern cultured buttermilk is different altogether. Cultured buttermilk is made by adding a bacterial culture to lowfat milk. Various controls determine whether the end result will be buttermilk, sour cream, yogurt or cheese. In England, cultured buttermilk is sold in plastic tubs or *pots* (like yogurt). It can be difficult to find although, at this writing, Sainsburys carry Raines' Live Cultured Buttermilk -- look for it near the yogurt. If you can't find any, you may substitute using one cup of yogurt for one cup of buttermilk in most recipes.
Cabbage, Chinese	*Chinese leaf* or *leaf cabbage*
Cabbage, green	*White cabbage* or *green cabbage*
Cake	*Cake* or *gâteau*
Cake, angel food	*Angel cake* Angel food cake or *angel cake* is a cake made with egg whites, cake flour, and sugar but with no fat.
Cake batter	*Cake mixture* The combined raw cake ingredients are usually referred to in American recipes as batter or cake batter.
Cake, devil's food	Devil's food cake is a rich, dark, moist, and dense chocolate cake. Its name stems from the fact that it's so rich and delicious it must be sinful.

Cake, pound	May substitute using *Madeira cake* Pound cake is a cake made of butter, sugar, flour and eggs and is so named because all the ingredients are measured by the pound. (*Cf* Cupcake.)
Cake, sheet	Technically speaking, a sheet cake is a single-layer cake baked in a 24" x 18" x 1" (*60cm* x *45cm* x *2.5cm*) pan; a half-sheet cake is one baked in an 18" x 12" x 1" pan (*45cm* x *30cm* x *2.5cm*). However, in the US the term "sheet cake" has come to mean any single-layer rectangular cake.
Cake pan, bundt	Use a Kugelhopf tin. Bundt pans are large fluted pans (usually 8½" [*21.5cm*] diameter) used for making dense cakes similar to pound cakes. Kugelhopf tins are typically an inch larger in diameter than bundt pans and may be substituted when making bundt cakes.
Cake pan, rectangular (for sheet cakes)	The typical size for rectangular cake pans is 13" x 9" x 2" (*33 x 23 x 5cm*). If you cannot find a tin cake pan this size, you may use a comparably-sized glass or enamel roasting pan. However, if you bake a cake in a glass or enamel roasting pan, lower the oven temperature by 25°F (*14°C* or ¼ gas mark).
Cake pan, round (for layer cakes)	*Round tin* or *sandwich tin* Americans use round cake pans for baking layer cakes. These cakes are normally two layers high, often frosted with a butter-based frosting, and are typically used for birthday cakes. The British more commonly use round

	tins for baking sponge cakes and *sponge sandwiches*.
Cake pan, spring-form	*Spring-clip tin*
Cake pan, tube	An angel food cake is baked in a plain, undecorated tube pan. You may substitute for the tube pan using a decoratively patterned Kugelhopf tin.
Calorie	*Kcal* American food labels list 'Calories' while British food labels list *Kj* (*Kilojoules*) and *Kcal* (*Kilocalories*). A Calorie (with a capital C) or a Kilocalorie equals the amount of heat necessary to raise the temperature of one litre of water by 1°C; a calorie (with a small c) will raise the temperature of a millilitre of water by 1°C. Calories are units of heat; joules are units of energy. A Kilojoule equals 1,000 joules or approximately 4.2 Calories (*Kcal*). And if you're counting calories, it's the *Kcal* amounts you need to add up.
Can	*Tin* or *can*
Can opener	*Tin opener*
Candied (e.g. candied ginger)	*Crystallized*
Candy	*Sweets* (or *chocolates*, if they're chocolate). In the UK, *candy* is a particular type of icing confection.
Candy bars	*Chocolate bars*

Candy, cotton	*Candy floss*
	Cotton candy or *candy floss* is a spun sugar confection traditionally sold at fair grounds and seaside resorts both in America and Britain.
Candy, hard	*Boiled sweets*
Candy shots or Non pareils	*Hundreds and thousands*
	These are the round multi-coloured tiny candy shots used to decorate cookies and cakes. They are known by a variety of names in the US but one name I have not heard them called there is *hundreds and thousands*.
Candy sprinkles or jimmies	*Non pareils* or *vermicelli*
	These are the elongated tiny candy sprinkles, usually chocolate, used to decorate cookies and cakes but especially used for ice cream toppings. These go by a variety of names in the US, including sprinkles, shots, jimmies.
Canning	*Bottling*
	In Britain, *canning* means just that - canning - using cans or tins. *Bottling* means bottling using bottles or jars. This distinction does not exist in the American home. Home canning in America normally uses bottles or jars.
Canning jars	*Bottling* or *preserving jars*
Celery	The light green celery sold throughout the US ('American green') is also sold in English supermarkets but the type of celery I see most often in the marketplace is a pale greenish-yellow variety, such as 'Golden self-blanching'. I mention this because the first time I

encountered the pale celery, I thought there was something wrong with it - there isn't. You may use either variety in any recipe calling for celery.

Celery root   *Celeriac*

Cereals, breakfast   Sugar Pops (US) are called *Sugar Puffs* (UK); Coco Puffs (US) are called *Coco Pops* (UK); Raisin Squares (US) are called *Raisin Splitz* in the UK. I won't list all the translations but suffice it to say you'll have to look carefully when buying breakfast cereal. Being aware breakfast cereal names are often different in England, I bought Kellogg's *Ricicles* thinking they were Rice Krispies. In fact, they were sugar-coated Rice Krispies. In England, Rice Krispies for one, goes by its American name.

Cheese, American   *'Singles' Processed Cheese* or *Kraft 'Singles' (cheese food)*
American cheese is a processed cheese, that is, its ripening process has been arrested at a given point by heat treatment. It is usually made from 1 or 2 cheese types which have been blended together. Processed cheese is very popular in America (accounting for an estimated third of the cheese produced there). Reasons for its popularity include the fact that it melts easily; is cheap; keeps well and is bland (and for this reason, popular with children). It is equally shunned by others who find it tastes more of the plastic in which it was wrapped than of a cheese. Sliced American cheese is available in British supermarkets as *Kraft*

'Singles' (cheese food) or *'Singles' Processed Cheese.*

Cheese, colby

Substitute using a mild cheddar.
Colby cheese is a mild, whole-milk cheddar which originated in Colby, Wisconsin in the late 1800s.

Cheese, cream

Soft cheese or *cream cheese* or *Philadelphia*

Cheese, farmer

See *Cheese, pot* this section.

Cheese food

Cheese food is cheese that's been processed with cream, milk, cheese whey or whey albumin; at least 51% of the product must be pure cheese according to US FDA regulations.

Cheese, Monterey Jack

Monterey Jack, a California cheddar, is a soft, delicate tasting cheese. You may substitute using a mild cheddar.

Cheese, Muenster

American Muenster cheese is a mild and bland cheese, very different from the full-bodied French Munster or the German Münster cheese (and should not be confused with them). For recipes calling for Muenster cheese, you may substitute using a mild cheddar.

Cheese, pot

Pot cheese, an ingredient called for in many Jewish recipes, is available from some speciality food shops and from Jewish delicatessens. It is made from milk fermenting naturally and is drier and less salty than cottage cheese. It goes well in strong flavoured dishes and also makes for a good filling for pastries, crêpes, and piroshki. If you cannot find pot cheese, you may substitute using ricotta, or the drier Indian cheese, paneer, or else farmer cheese (if you can find it). Pot cheese and its substitutes do not store well. Tightly wrapped and refrigerated, they'll keep for only about one week. (To make paneer, see the recipe on page 213.)

Cheese, ricotta   Ricotta cheese is now available in many supermarkets in England. If you cannot find ricotta, you may substitute using paneer (recipe on page 213). Alternatively, cottage cheese may be used after it's been wrapped in cheesecloth (*muslin*) and hung to drain.

Cheese, sharp   *Mature cheese*

Cheese, Swiss   use *Gruyère*
Gruyère is made in Switzerland and France and is commonly available at cheese stalls and in supermarkets. Gruyère is slightly sharper than the American Emmentaler known as Swiss. You won't find a cheese in England called Swiss cheese, per se.

Cheese Whiz   *Cheese Spread*, which comes in a shallow tub, is a reasonable substitute.
Cheese Whiz is a pasteurised processed cheese sauce, available in jars and aerosol cans, and normally used to decorate crackers and other hors d'oeuvres. It is sometimes called for in recipes.

Cheesecloth   *Muslin* or *butter muslin*
Muslin is available from fabric shops in the UK -- not in supermarkets (like in the US).

Cherries, candied   *Glacé cherries*

Cherries, maraschino   *Cocktail cherries (with maraschino flavouring)*

Chicken livers   Chicken livers are available from kosher butchers and from poulterers. Now and then, tubs of frozen chicken livers are available from supermarkets.

Chicken liver, chopped   You may use *Chicken liver paté* as a substitute.

Chicken quarter or portion   *Chicken joint*

Chicory   *Endive* (curly-leaved)
Curly endive has frilly, bitter-tasting, dark-green narrow leaves that curl at the edges.

Chiles, jalapeño   Jalapeño chiles or peppers are extremely hot. They are used in many Mexican and Tex-Mex dishes and are widely available throughout the southwest US. Jars of pickled jalapeños are available in England from some supermarkets.

Chinese parsley   *Coriander leaves*
See listing for Cilantro.

Chitterlings   Chitterlings (pron. chit' lins) are made from pig's stomach and intestines which have been cleaned, cut-up, and cooked like tripe. In England, the stomach and intestines are normally removed from the animal before they reach the butcher so finding ingredients for American chitterlings will be difficult here. The word *chitterlings* in England refers to sausages made from bits of intestine; these sausages are normally grilled and served with a vinaigrette dressing.

Chocolate, dark

Plain chocolate
If you want a dark chocolate candy bar, ask for a *plain chocolate bar*.

Chocolate, semi-sweet baking

Plain chocolate or *bittersweet chocolate*
You may use a *plain chocolate bar* from the sweets aisle for any recipes calling for semi-sweet chocolate.

Chocolate, unsweetened baking

Bitter chocolate
Bitter chocolate is not normally available in supermarkets although some speciality shops do carry it. To substitute for 1 ounce of unsweetened chocolate, use 3 tablespoons (*45ml*) cocoa plus 1 tablespoon (*15ml*) butter or fat.

Cider, apple

Non-alcoholic sweet apple cider is not widely available in England. However, some English health food shops and supermarkets carry apple juices which have been made from crushed apples and taste very similar to American apple cider. In the US, sweet apple cider is made from ground or crushed raw apples which are pressed to extract their juice, while apple juice is made from cooked apples (or from cider that's been clarified and heated to keep it sweet). Also see *Hard cider*.

Cider, hard

Cider
Hard cider is sweet cider which has been allowed to ferment and become alcoholic. In America, hard cider is a brownish and sometimes cloudy drink sold primarily at apple

orchards in the fall; it is a seasonal drink. In England, alcoholic cider (called simply *cider*) is sold year round and is a major industry. It is available everywhere that beer and wine are sold. Many of the English *ciders* are carbonated and clear, resembling sparkling wine.[3]

Cilantro[4]   *Coriander leaves*

Citrons   *Mixed peel* or *candied peel*

Clams   Categories of American clam include Atlantic hard-shell and soft-shell, and Pacific hard-shell.
Atlantic hard-shell clams:
Size: 1½"-4½" (*4-11cm*) across.
Types: 'Little necks' (the smallest and most tender); 'cherrystone' (medium-sized) -- both are suitable for eating raw on the half-shell and for steaming. 'Chowders' (4½") and the deep-sea clams called 'surf clams' and 'ocean quahogs' (also 4½") are chopped and then canned or frozen, and are used for making clam chowder.
Pacific hard-shell clams:
Size: 1-2" (*2.5-5cm*) across.
Types: 'Littlenecks' (one word -- sometimes called 'rock clams') and 'Manilas' -- these clams are usually steamed.
Atlantic soft-shell clams:
Size: Up to 2" (*5cm*) across.
Atlantic soft-shell clams are also called

---

[3] To be classed a cider, the alcohol content must be between 1.2 and 8.4%.

[4] Cilantro is the Spanish word for coriander leaves. In areas of the US with a large Spanish-speaking population, e.g. Los Angeles, coriander leaves are known by all as *cilantro*.

'longnecks'; 'belly clams'; 'steamers'; and 'Ipswitch' and are served fried, steamed or raw. Hard-shell clams are cultivated in Britain but most are exported to France and Belgium. If you cannot find clams locally, you may substitute using cockles or oysters for raw clams on the half-shell recipes; cockles or mussels for steamed clam recipes; and mussels for fried clam recipes.

Clam chowder, Manhattan	Manhattan clam chowder is a water and tomato-based clam soup containing clams, bacon, onions, carrots, celery, potatoes and herbs. As of this writing, Manhattan clam chowder is not available in the supermarkets here.
Clam chowder, New England	Clam chowder originated in France many centuries ago and got its name from the pot the chowder was cooked in -- *la chaudière*. It migrated to Canada and from there to New England. New England clam chowder is a water and milk-based soup containing clams, salt pork, onion and potatoes. When people refer to clam chowder, they usually mean New England clam chowder. As of this writing, New England clam chowder is not available in English supermarkets, although other milk-based fish chowders are.
Club soda	*Sparkling water* or *fizzy water*
Coconut, dried shredded	*Desiccated coconut*
Cold cuts	Cold cuts refers to sliced sandwich meats and cheese. A typical plate of cold cuts might

include sliced salami, ham, roast beef, bologna, and various cheeses.

Collard greens

Kale, spring greens (e.g., beet, kohlrabi) and collard greens may be interchanged in recipes. (NB: Seakale is different from kale.)

Colostrum
or firstlings

Beestings
This is the first milk a mammal gives after the birth of young. It is not something which is normally sold, here or in the US.

Cookie

Biscuit
Although *biscuits* is the English word for what Americans call 'cookies', *biscuits* in England more often refers to a sweet that is a cross between a candy bar and a small cake. Some American-style cookies are now available in England and these are labelled as *cookies* -- not *biscuits*. (To make the quintessential American cookie, see the recipe for chocolate chip cookies on page 177.)

Cookie cutter

Pastry cutter or *cookie cutter*
The variety of shapes of *pastry cutters* available is sometimes limited to round, fluted-round and gingerbreadman. For a greater variety of shapes, check the kitchen and hardware shops.

Cookie sheet

Baking tray or *baking sheet.*

Cool Whip

Whipped topping
Cool Whip is the name brand of a popular whipped topping sold in the US. It comes in tubs and aerosol cans, and is used in place of

whipped cream. Similar products in England include *Real Dairy Cream Swirls* (a dairy product) and *Delissimo* (a blend of skimmed milk and vegetable oil). I've included this entry for the same reason I've included Crisco: American recipes often use the name brand in place of the thing itself, saying '½ cup of Crisco' (rather than shortening) or 'top with Cool Whip' (rather than whipped cream).

Coriander leaves

You can buy large bunches of *coriander leaves* from Indian (*Asian*) shops. Supermarkets often carry them, but in much smaller quantities (and at a much higher price). Also, as many corner shops are Asian-owned, it's not unusual to find the fresh leaves sold there as well.

Corn

Sweetcorn; maize
Sweetcorn or *maize* is the British term for what Americans call *corn* or *corn on the cob*. In Great Britain, the word *corn* refers to a particular grain and, depending on where you are, that grain differs. In England, *corn* means wheat; in Scotland, *corn* means oats. So if someone refers to a field of corn, you'll need to know in which country it is in order to know which grain they mean.

Corn chips

Corn chips are a crunchy snack food similar to tortilla chips. Corn chips are not commonly available in British supermarkets but tortilla chips are.

Corn, creamed

Creamed or cream-style corn is sometimes available in supermarkets, but never when you need it for a recipe. To make creamed corn from a can of regular corn, see the recipe on page 161.

Corn oil

Corn oil or *maize oil*
Corn oil is expressed from the germ of *maize* and is widely available in England.

Corn syrup, dark

Dark corn syrup is not available in British supermarkets. It has a flavour midway between caramel and molasses so a ¼ *treacle* to ¾ *glucose syrup* mix would be an approximate substitute as regards taste, but not sweetness. *Glucose syrup* is twice as sweet as corn syrup so if you substitute using *glucose syrup*, you'll need to decrease the amounts of other sugars called for in the recipe, otherwise you'll end up with a sickly-sweet concoction. Dark corn syrup is available in some speciality food shops (for addresses, see the *Mail Order and Shopping Guide* section).

Corn syrup, light

Light corn syrup is not available in British supermarkets but it is available in some speciality food shops. The closest substitute in taste is *liquid glucose* or *glucose syrup*, available from chemists (Boots keep it behind the counter) and some health food shops. *Glucose syrup* comes in a jar (usually between *250g-454g*) and can range in price from a little more than what you'd pay for corn syrup in the US to virtually three times as much. (The cheapest one I've found was from a health food stall.) *Glucose syrup* is also more viscous than corn syrup (understatement) so to loosen it, run the jar under hot water; to stir it, add a spoon or more of just-boiled water until it's the right

*British glucose syrup and
American corn syrup.*

*American molasses and
dark corn syrup.*

consistency. Also, whereas corn syrup has half
the sweetening power of sugar,[5] *glucose syrup*
tastes equally as sweet as sugar so, when
substituting *glucose syrup* for corn syrup,
lessen the amount of other sugars or sweet
syrups called for in the recipe.
(Note: *Maize malt syrup* is <u>not</u> corn syrup.)

Corned beef
(fresh only)

Salt beef or *cooked brisket*
In England, *corned beef* normally refers to
cooked pieces of cured beef packed in their
gelatinous material and fat and then pressed or
moulded in a tin. In the US, corned beef refers

---

[5] The sweetness of 1 cup of corn syrup is equal to that of 1/2 cup of sugar.

to both the tinned corned beef as well as whole pieces of *salted beef*. The *salted beef* is used whole in recipes such as corned beef and cabbage, or thinly sliced for Reubens. (To make Reuben sandwiches, see the recipe on page 147.)

Cornmeal	*Polenta, maize meal, cornmeal.* For American recipes calling for cornmeal, use a coarsely ground polenta. Fine and coarse polenta is available in many Indian (*Asian*) groceries as well as in some health food shops. Italian polenta is coarsely ground; West Indian cornmeal comes in fine and coarse ground.
Cornstarch	*Cornflour*
Crackers	*Savoury biscuits*
Cracker crumbs	When an American recipe calls for cracker crumbs, use crushed, savoury, salted biscuits (e.g., TUC Biscuits). However, if it calls for Graham cracker crumbs, substitute using crushed digestive biscuits.
Cracklin' or crackling	In Britain, *cracklings* refer to the crisp roasted skin of a pig. In the US, it refers to the crisp roasted skin of either a pig or a chicken. In Jewish cooking, it *always* refers to chicken skin.
Cranberries	Prepared cranberry sauce is available in jars from many supermarkets. Also, in late November or early December (and continuing through to Christmas) fresh cranberries are available in supermarkets. To make your own cranberry sauce, see the recipe on page 168.

Crawfish, crayfish	*Crayfish* In Louisiana, crayfish is known both as 'crawfish' and 'crawdads'. Crayfish is a freshwater crustacean, similar to a small lobster; in France it is known as *écrevisses*.
Cream Chart	*See page 119.*
Cream, heavy	*Whipping cream* American heavy cream (or heavy whipping cream) has a fat content between 36-40%. English *whipping cream* may be substituted as it contains about 38% fat.
Cream, light or coffee cream	*Single cream* *Single cream* contains about 18% fat; American light cream contains between 18% and 30% fat.
Cream, sour	*Soured cream* or *sour cream* *Soured cream* is available in some supermarkets. If you cannot locate it, you can make your own, provided you don't need it the same day. To make your own, pour 8 ounces (*240 ml*) of *single cream* into a litre jar. Add 5 teaspoons (*25 ml*) of a starter (e.g., cottage cheese), cover the jar and shake it vigorously. Stir in a further 8 oz. (*240 ml*) of *single cream*, cover the jar and let it stand 24 hours at *25-30°* *C* (75-80°F). Otherwise, if you need the sour cream straight away, you can make 'imitation' sour cream by stirring lemon juice (or a drop or two of vinegar) into cream (it's imitation because its sourness is due to citric acid rather than lactic acid). Also see Addendum, p. 227.

Cream of wheat cereal, commonly used in America as baby food.

Cream, whipping

Whipping cream
If you can't find *whipping cream*, use equal parts *single cream* and *double cream*. English whipping cream has a fat content of about 38%. American light whipping cream has a fat content between 30-36%. (See Cream Chart on page 119.)

Cream of wheat

Cream of wheat is finely cracked wheat, usually with the bran and germ removed. It is prepared as a hot cereal and is especially popular as a baby food. Cream of wheat is not available in supermarkets here but it is available in some speciality food shops. For addresses, see the *Mail Order and Shopping Guide* section.

Creamer	*Milk jug* or *creamer*
Crêpe	*Pancake* or *crêpe*
Crisco	Crisco is a well-known brandname of shortening sold in America. I've included it because it's become synonymous with the word shortening. (See *Shortening* entry.)
Crumbs, cracker	Use crushed, savoury, salted biscuits (e.g., TUC biscuits).
Crumbs, Graham cracker	Substitute using crushed digestive biscuits.
Crumbs, Italian bread	Use seasoned, dried bread crumbs. Italian bread crumbs may be made by adding to each cup of dried bread crumbs the following:

       3 Tablespoons grated Parmesan cheese
       ¼ teaspoon basil
       ½ teaspoon chives
       ½ teaspoon oregano.

Cucumber — The type of cucumber that's commonly sold in England is the long 'hot house' variety, and it's sold whole and/or cut in half. The type of cucumber most commonly sold in America, and the type referred to in American cookbooks, is a shorter cucumber (avg. 7" [*18cm*]) with a waxed skin, and larger seeds than the hot-house variety. When using an English cucumber in an American recipe, remember to only use a 7" piece when a whole cucumber is called for. Also, when using the hot-house variety you won't need to seed or peel the cucumber, should the American recipe call for that.

Cupcakes	*Fairy cakes* Cupcakes, little muffin-sized cakes (normally baked in a muffin pan), got their name from their ingredients being measured by the cupful.
Cymling (squash)	*Custard squash* Cymling is more commonly referred to in the US as 'patty pan'.
Danish or Danish pastry	A Danish is a rich, flaky, yeasted pastry containing a sweet filling. The dough is folded over the filling and is usually glazed with a sugar syrup. Typical fillings include prune, apple, or cheese.
Dessert	*Afters* or *sweet* or *pudding* Despite the fact that the dessert might be pie, people will still ask 'What's for pud (or pudding)?' And also, whereas in the US desserts are eaten with a dessert fork (unless they're something that actually requires a spoon, like ice cream), in England, they're normally eaten with a large spoon.
Dinner	*Tea* or *dinner* In America, dinner usually means the main meal eaten at night. In England, the main night-time meal is often referred to as *tea*. Even when feeding the cat, people refer to it as *giving the cat her tea*. *Dinner*, in England, means the main meal of the day whether served at night or mid-day.
Dish detergent	*Washing up liquid*

Doggie bag	If you cannot finish a restaurant meal, you may ask for a "doggie bag" and your leftovers will be wrapped to go. But whereas in the US, asking for a doggie bag is considered the norm (and indeed, a compliment to the chef), in England asking for a doggie bag invites looks bordering on disgust, as if you were asking them to retrieve and wrap something from the bin. In one restaurant, they were clearly so unused to people requesting a doggie bag that I got mine in an enormous plastic tub which I now use as a cookie container (an entire batch of cookies fits in it!). I can only assume that the English reaction stems from an old tradition of leaving a bit on your plate for the help but as that no longer applies (what's left on your plate now goes in the bin), and especially if the food was good, why throw it out?
Dough, yeast	American recipes instruct you to *punch down* yeast dough while British recipes tell you to *knock back* the dough. Also, in England the second rising of the dough is referred to as letting the dough *prove*. This is different from letting the yeast proof. (See *Proof* entry.)
Dressing, French	*French dressing* or *vinaigrette* There are two types of French dressing sold in the US. The clear vinaigrette (the less common of the two in the US) is widely available throughout England. The more common French dressing sold in America is an orange-coloured, slightly viscous dressing and, as of this writing, is not sold in England. (To make your own, see the French dressing recipe on page 143.)

Dressing, Russian	Russian dressing can be difficult to find in England. You can either substitute using Thousand Island dressing, which is similar, or else make your own (for recipe, see page 144).
Dressing, salad	*Salad Cream* In the US, 'salad dressing' can refer to a particular a type of salad dressing (such as French or Thousand Island), or it can refer specifically to the dressing called 'salad dressing'. This is a *salad cream* type of dressing which is essentially the same as mayonnaise but does not contain egg yolks, and is a little sweeter-tasting than mayonnaise. Note: When eating out, salads often do not come with dressing. And if you ask for dressing, your choice (in the Midlands, anyway) is often limited to *salad cream*.
Dressing, turkey	*Stuffing*
Dutch oven	*Flameproof casserole* or *iron camp oven* In America, a Dutch oven refers to a large, heavy pot or kettle, often of cast iron, and with a tight-fitting lid. It is used for slow-cooking.
Egg beater	*Rotary whisk* or *egg beater*
Eggplant	*Aubergine*
Egg noodles	*Tagliatelle*
Egg roll	*Spring roll*
Eggs, white-shelled	All the hens' eggs I have seen in England have been brown-shelled. I asked an egg-seller where I could get white-shelled eggs to colour

for Easter and she told me she'd not seen white-shelled hens' eggs in years. (White-shelled duck eggs are available from egg sellers but they're more resistant to food colouring, resulting in streaky colours.) Note: there is no difference in nutrition between brown and white hens' eggs.

Electric beater
or electric mixer

Electric whisk or *hand mixer*

Enchilada

Enchiladas are a Mexican dish made from soft corn tortillas. The tortillas are wrapped around a spicy sauce containing tomatoes, chili, cumin, onion, and meat or beans. The wrapped tortillas are placed alongside one another in a casserole dish, topped with sauce and shredded cheese, and baked.

Endive
(or Belgian endive)

Chicory
This is also known as Brussels chicory, Belgian endive, French endive, and *witloof* (white leaf). *Chicory* is a head of tightly-packed, light-coloured leaves with yellowish-green tips -- the pale colour is achieved through a growing technique known as 'blanching', that is, being grown in the dark. A head of *chicory* is small (about 6" [*15cm*] long), cigar-shaped, and has a somewhat bitter taste. It may be eaten raw (as in a salad) or cooked.

Escarole

Batavia, batavia endive or *escarole*
Batavia, a variety of endive, has wide but curvy, light-green leaves and resembles a lettuce whose leaves have exploded into a haphazard curly mass. Its flavour is milder

than that of Belgian endive. Though it is not commonly available in England, some speciality food shops do carry it. For addresses, see the *Mail Order and Shopping Guide* section.

Extract (e.g., vanilla extract)	*Essence* (e.g., *essence of vanilla*)
Fast food	*Take-away foods*
Faucet	*Tap*
Fettucine	*Vermicelli*
Filbert	If you cannot find filberts, use *cob nuts* or *hazelnuts. Cob nuts* and *filberts* are cultivated; *hazelnuts* grow wild. See *hazelnuts.*
Fish sticks	*Fish fingers*
Flan	*Créme caramel*
Flounder	Substitute using *plaice* Flounder is a flat fish of the same family as plaice. Plaice, a good eating fish, is caught in the North Sea and is available throughout the year.
Flour, all purpose	*Plain flour*
Flour, bread or hard-wheat	*Strong flour*
Flour, cake	*Soft* or *softgrain flour* or *cake flour* (also known as *weak flour* and *household flour*)
Flour, self-rising	*Self-raising flour*

Flour, wholewheat	Substitute using *wholemeal flour*, a more coarsely ground flour than wholewheat.
Flowerets	*Florets*
French fries	*Chips*
Frosting	*Icing* Sainsbury's carry small plastic containers of *soft icing*, and Safeway have just started carrying Betty Crocker's prepared frosting. You can also get blocks of *cake covering* (which you melt down for icing), but the ones I've tried were disappointing. (To make your own frosting, see recipe on page 211.)
Fruitcake	To get the type of cake Americans call fruit cake, ask for either *rich fruitcake* or *Christmas cake*. Asking for *fruitcake* will get you a moist yellow cake laced with currants and cherries.
Fruit pitter	*Fruit stoner*
Garlic press	*Garlic crusher*
Gefilte fish	Gefilte fish (Yiddish for 'filled fish') are balls of a chopped fish mixture, cooked in broth and usually served chilled. Gefilte fish is available in jars from Jewish delicatessens and from some speciality food shops.
Ginger ale	Ginger ale and ginger beer are both commonly available in England. Ginger ale is made from adding ginger essence to carbonated water while ginger beer is made from fermenting ginger root and sugar, and is much spicier than ginger ale.

Ginger root	*Root ginger* as well as *ginger root.*
Golden Fruit Raisin Biscuits	*Garibaldi* In a sense, this is a reverse entry. *Garibaldi* are a very popular British biscuit and everyone here knows what a *Garibaldi* is. Golden Fruit Raisin Biscuits are also very popular in the US and everyone knows them by sight but, unlike *Garibaldi*, no one ever remembers their name. I've included this entry to help those struggling to remember a catchy name that doesn't exist; they're simply called Golden Fruit Raisin Biscuits in the US.
Graham crackers	Sylvester Graham (1794-1851) for whom the graham cracker was named, was an American nutritionist who insisted that the bread and biscuits sold under his name be made with flour containing all the original bran. Graham crackers are available in some speciality food shops but if they're called for in a recipe, just use *digestive biscuits* instead. (For a mock graham cracker crust recipe, see page 213.)
Granola	*Muesli* is very similar. Although *muesli* is not exactly the same as granola, their ingredients are very nearly identical. Both are made with rolled oats (and other grains), nuts, and dried fruit. In addition to these, granola usually contains brown sugar (or honey), oil, and spices such as cinnamon or nutmeg; and the *muesli* ingredients may also include fresh fruit and yogurt (or milk). The main difference lies in the fact that granola is toasted in an oven while *muesli's* ingredients are

simply combined or soaked overnight in milk or yogurt.

Green onions

Spring onions or *salad onions*

Grill (verb)

When an American recipe says to grill something, it means to dry-cook it on a grill (e.g., barbecue grill), under which there are burning coals or other fuel. If you don't have a barbecue, you may cook the food in the stove's broiler (the *grill* of the *cooker*, UK). The only difference will be the heat will be coming from above what's being cooked rather than from below it.

Grinder

Baguette (with a filling)
The term 'grinder' is used in New England and is another word for 'submarine sandwich'. According to *The Dictionary of American Food and Drink* by John Mariani, the term stems from the amount of chewing needed to 'grind through' the sandwich. Also see the submarine sandwich entry on page 100.

Grits

Grits are not commonly available in England (nor for that matter are they commonly available in the US other than in the South). Grits are the broken grains of hominy (hominy is corn with the hull and germ removed). Grits are served with butter, like mashed potato. If you have a grain mill, you can make your own grits by coarsely grinding dried hominy (or hard flint corn or popcorn). When buying grits, be sure to check for bugs. If you see any tiny webs on or in the package, don't buy them; it means they have bugs. I mention this because it is something grits are prone to. Grits are available in some speciality food shops; for addresses, see the *Mail Order and Shopping Guide* section.

Gumbo	Gumbo (from the African word for 'okra') is a Creole stew containing okra, tomatoes, onion, smoked ham, and either chicken, seafood, or meat.
Half & half	*Half cream* *Half cream* is very difficult to find so if, like me, you cannot locate *half cream*, then mix equal parts *single cream* and milk. Half & half is most commonly used in the US in coffee. It is half milk and half cream and, although its fat content can go as high as 18%, its average fat content is between 10.5% - 11.7%, roughly the same as that of *half cream*.
Hamburger	*Beefburger* During the BSE crisis in the 1990s, there were some in England who had sworn off beef but who continued to eat *ham*burgers in the mistaken belief they were made of ham.
Hamburger buns	*Baps* or *plain tea cakes* or, more recently (adopted from American), *buns.*
Hard sauce	*Rum butter* or *brandy butter* Hard sauce is a combination of butter, sugar, and usually some type of alcohol. It is traditionally served on cake or pudding.
Hash brown potatoes	Hash browns are an American dish made from diced potatoes which are pan-fried until browned.

Packaged grits, above. Grits, cooked and uncooked, below.

Hazelnuts	Use *hazelnuts, cob nuts,* or *filberts. Hazelnuts* are round and very small, and grow wild in southern England. The ready-shelled nuts sold here which are labelled *hazelnuts* are often, in fact, *cob nuts* or *filberts.*
Head cheese	*Brawn* (For more information, see the head cheese entry on page 83 in the Pork section.)
Hearts of palm	*Hearts of palm* or *palm hearts* Hearts of palm are now available from many British supermarkets.
Hoagie	See *Submarine sandwich.*
Home fries	Home fries are sliced raw potatoes sautéed with onion and cooked until well-browned. Those large breakfasts served in American restaurants and diners wouldn't be anywhere near as popular as they are if it weren't for the home fries that come with them. For a recipe for home fries, see page 163.
Hors d'oeuvre	*Starter*
Hot dog tongs	*Serving tongs* or *kitchen tongs* or *tongs*
Ice cream	Ice cream goes by the same name in England as in America but there are differences. Ice cream sold in the US typically has less air whipped into it, creating a denser ice cream (and less shrinkage when it melts). Also, almost all US ice cream is *dairy* ice cream, based on butterfat. In England, however, the biggest ice cream market is the *non-dairy* or vegetable fat ice cream (i.e., based on non-milk fats such as

American Jello (powdered) and English jelly (gelatinous block).

palm or coconut oil). When looking for an American-style ice cream, pick up a farmhouse dairy ice cream or a supermarket's 'luxury' brand of dairy ice cream; these are less aerated than most other English ice creams, and are the type that should be used when an American recipe calls for ice cream.

Indian

Asian
In America, people from India are called Indians while the term 'Asian' usually means someone from Japan or China. In England, *Asian* usually refers to someone from India or Pakistan. So, if you are directed to the *Asian* market, don't go looking for a Chinese grocery; they mean the Indian shop.

Jambalaya	Jambalaya is a Cajun-Creole tomato-based stew and usually contains ham, seafood (and/or chicken), green pepper, rice, and seasonings.
Jawbreakers	*Gobstoppers*
Jello	*Jelly* In the US, this is sold in a powdered form; in the UK it's sold in a gelatinous block, wrapped in plastic and usually boxed. (*See photo, previous page.*)
Jelly, grape	I have not seen grape jelly in the supermarkets but it is available from some speciality food shops.
Jelly roll (or roll cake)	*Swiss roll*
Jelly roll pan	*Swiss roll tin* The American jelly roll pan is typically 1" (*25mm*) deep while the *Swiss roll tin* is usually ¾" (*19mm*) deep.
Jewish food	Many American grocery stores have a Jewish food section but English supermarkets tend not to (unless they're in a Jewish quarter). To find Jewish food (e.g., kosher salt; half-sour pickles; fresh bagels; etc.), find the Jewish quarter of the city nearest you and go to a kosher butcher shop, delicatessen, or supermarket there. (Kosher butchers often carry a full range of Jewish foods - not just meats.) For the Jewish section of Manchester, go to Whitefield; for Birmingham, go to Mosley; and for London, look in Golders Green and Edgeware.

Custard made from rennet liquid.

(Remember kosher butchers and delis are closed on Saturdays.)

Jicama

Jicama (pronounced hik' a ma) is a Mexican root vegetable with the crispness and whiteness of a white radish but with a pleasant flavour all its own. Jicama is often peeled and cut up as part of a vegetable dip (*crudités*). You may substitute for jicama using white radish but this will lack jicama's subtle sweet taste.

Junket rennet custard

Rennet liquid
In the US, Junket rennet custard is sold in boxes in powdered form. It makes a smooth, thin custard when combined with milk. Junket

Kasha uncooked.

rennet custard is not sold in England but rennet liquid is, and you can make the custard from this (see recipe, p. 198). Rennet liquid is available (or may be ordered) from certain chemists, speciality food shops, and some supermarkets (currently Safeway carry it).

Kasha

Roasted buckwheat or *buckwheat groats*
Kasha is the Russian name for buckwheat groats. Although kasha is treated as a grain, botanically it is a fruit in the rhubarb family and as such, offers an alternative to those sensitive to or allergic to wheat. Kasha may be eaten as a cereal, a side dish, or as part of a main dish. Always use roasted buckwheat unless cooking it for cereal. (NB Cream of

buckwheat may not be substituted.) In the US, kasha is usually found in the Jewish food section of the supermarkets. In England it is available in Jewish delis and butchers, and in many health food shops. (See *Jewish food*, this section.)

Ketchup   *Tomato sauce* or *tomato ketchup*

Lamb cuts   *See page 57.*

Lasagne noodles   The name is the same but the noodles are not. The lasagne sold in England is shorter than its American counterpart and, whereas English lasagne typically is flat, most lasagne sold in the US has fluted edging. Also, the only lasagne I've seen in England is the type that 'requires no pre-cooking' and the only one I've ever seen in the US is the kind that must be boiled first. (*See photos, following page.*)

Legumes   *Pulses*
                            Pulses are leguminous plants whose seeds are used as a vegetable (this includes peas, beans, lentils, soy beans, and peanuts).

Lemonade   *Homemade* or *fresh lemonade*
                            When the British say *lemonade*, they mean a carbonated lemon-flavoured soft drink, also called *sparkling lemonade*. The type of lemonade sold in the US is called *homemade or fresh lemonade*. As of this writing, Safeway stock a boxed drink called 'Traditional style lemon crush' which is very similar to American lemonade. (To make your own, see the lemonade recipe on page 209.)

Above: Green and wholewheat lasagne from Safeway in England
(Safeway in England is no longer connected with Safeway in the US).
Below: Typical American lasagne.

LAMB CUTS

Something that never fails to impress visiting Americans is the vast number of sheep grazing here, and it is little wonder. In the US, lamb is probably the least-consumed meat: in 1992, Americans ate the equivalent of 66.4 pounds of beef per person; 53.2 pounds of pork per person, and only *one* pound of lamb per person (and that pound probably at Eastertime). So, although there are quite a few American cuts of lamb listed here, not many Americans will have tried them.

Many of the popular cuts of lamb in England are different from the popular US cuts, so when my description of an American cut does not include an equivalent British cut, tell your butcher the section of the animal the cut is from and see if he can suggest an alternate cut. As American and British butchers cut up a sheep somewhat differently, I've included illustrations showing the differences.

By the way, the thin, papery skin that surrounds lamb chops, steaks, and roasts is known as the 'fell', and should be left on roasts when cooking (to hold their shape) but removed from steaks and chops.

NOTE: When viewing the BRITISH LAMB CUTS diagram that follows, bear in mind that Scottish and English lamb is not cut exactly the same. In Scotland, a shoulder is cut as a larger joint, and includes part of the neck and the breast. This shoulder joint is then divided into 2 or 3 joints, which are often boned, stuffed, and rolled into roasts. Also, the Scottish leg of lamb is cut differently from the English in that the Scottish cut includes the *chump* end of the loin. And their former French influence is still evident: the Scottish leg of lamb is called *gigot*. *Gigot* is usually divided into 3 sections: *chump*, *centre*, and *knuckle*.

LAMB CUTS, *cont.*

AMERICAN LAMB CUTS

LOIN

RIB (or RACK)

SHOULDER

NECK

LEG

Sir- loin end

HIND SHANK

HIND SHANK

FORESHANK

LAMB CUTS, *cont.*

BRITISH LAMB CUTS

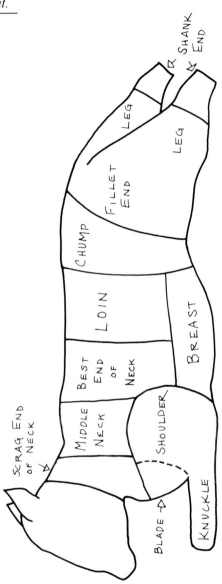

LAMB CUTS, *cont.*

Breast of lamb

The lamb breast is a very fatty, oblong cut of meat containing the ribs. In the US, it's often boned and trimmed of fat, then rolled and tied and sold as rolled breast or, if it's stuffed as well, sold as stuffed breast. In England, the cut called *rolled breast* is normally already stuffed. Breast of lamb is suitable for roasting or, provided it's well-trimmed of fat, braising.

Crown roast

This roast is from the rib or rack (*best end of neck*) section and is constructed by tying together 2 racks of trimmed ribs (*2 trimmed best ends*), and shaped to form a crown. To have one prepared, you will need to give your butcher a few days' notice.

Frenched leg of lamb

This is the same as the leg of lamb, but with the shank bone exposed: meat is cut away from the lower end of the leg so that an inch or so of the shank bone protrudes. It is suitable for roasting.

Frenched rib chops

French lamb cutlets
These chops from the rib or rack (*best end of neck*) section of the sheep contain rib eye muscle and a rib bone, the end of which is trimmed of meat. They are suitable for broiling (*grilling*), pan-broiling, and frying.

Lamb neck slices

In the US, these cuts are also known as lamb shoulder neck slices; lamb neck; and lamb for stew, bone in. They are round slices cut from the neck, containing a cross section of the neck bone, and are suitable for braising.

LAMB CUTS, *cont.*

Lamb patties

Lamb patties or lamburgers are just hamburgers made from lamb instead of beef. They may be made from any cut of ground (*minced*) lamb or its trimmings, and shaped into patties. They are fried or broiled, the same as a beef hamburger.

Lamb shank

This cut, also known in the US as lamb foreshank and lamb trotter, is the foreshank (or *knuckle*) end of the arm or front leg and contains the round leg bone. It is suitable for braising and cooking in liquid.

Leg chop

Leg fillet
These steaks from the sirloin end (*fillet end*) of the leg are suitable for broiling (*grilling*) and frying.

Leg of lamb, whole

Leg of lamb (also known in the US as leg roast, sirloin on) includes the sirloin section of the leg (with the hip bone) and the shank portion of the leg (with the round leg bone). Since sheep in the US are often slaughtered at a later age than British sheep, an American leg of lamb might weigh anywhere from 4½ - 9 pounds while a typical British leg of lamb weighs between 4 - 5½ pounds. Boned and cubed leg of lamb is commonly used for shish kebab.

Leg, shank half

The shank half (*knuckle end* or *shank end*) is the lower half of the hind leg and contains the round leg bone. This heavily muscled cut has a covering of fat and fell, and is suitable for roasting or braising.

LAMB CUTS, *cont.*

Leg, sirloin or
butt end

Fillet of lamb
This is the sirloin end (*fillet end*) of the leg and
is suitable for roasting.

Loin chops

These chops from the loin section are roughly
equivalent to the English cut of the same name.
They contain loin and tenderloin, usually with a
T-shaped bone separating the two, and are
suitable for broiling (*grilling*) and pan-broiling.

Rib chops or
rack lamb chops

Best end chops or
Best end of neck cutlets (or chops)
These chops are from the rib or rack (*best end
of neck*) section of the sheep and contain rib eye
muscle and a rib bone. They are suitable for
broiling (*grilling*), pan-broiling, and frying.

Rib roast, rack
roast, or rib rack

Roast joint
The lamb rib roast is from the rib or rack (*best
end of neck*) section of the sheep. It contains
rib bones, backbone, and thick, meaty rib eye
muscle. When the rib eye muscle is removed
from the rack and sliced into thick steaks, these
slices are known as medallions, and are suitable
for sautéing.

Riblets

Lamb riblets, also known in the US as breast
riblets, are long and narrow 1-1½" cuts from
the breast section, containing the rib bone.
They are suitable for braising, broiling
(*grilling*), and cooking in liquid.

Rolled loin roast

This is the loin roast but with the T-bone
removed, and then rolled and tied.

LAMB CUTS, *cont.*

Rolled shoulder
This is a cut from the shoulder, boned, rolled, and tied. It is suitable for roasting and braising.

Saddle
When the whole loin section is cut out in one saddle-shaped piece, consisting of both loins and often with the kidneys tied in with it, this is known as a saddle. (The name is the same in the US and in the UK.) This large roast (average weight 8 lbs.) requires slow roasting and if you intend to order one, your butcher will need a few days' notice to prepare it.

Saratoga chops
Saratoga chops are slices from the shoulder which are boned, rolled, and then skewered (to keep them from unrolling). They are suitable for braising and cooking in liquid.

Shoulder arm chop, arm cut, or round bone chop
The lamb shoulder arm chop is cut from the shoulder and contains the round arm bone. It is suitable for braising, broiling (*grilling*), and pan-broiling.

Shoulder blade chop
This cut, also known in the US as blade cut chops, is cut from the shoulder and contains the blade bone. It is suitable for braising, broiling (*grilling*), and frying.

Sirloin chops
These chops are roughly equivalent to English *chump chops* and come from the sirloin (*chump*) section of the sheep. They contain a portion of the hip bone, and are suitable for broiling (*grilling*) and braising.

Lettuce, Boston or butterhead	*Round lettuce* or *flat lettuce* Butterhead is the most commonly available lettuce in England and it's usually labelled *round* or *flat lettuce* -- you can get it in any market or supermarket.
Lettuce, romaine	*Cos lettuce* Romaine lettuce is the lettuce used in Caesar salads.
Liquor, hard	*Spirits*
Liverwurst	*Liver sausage* (or, *liver pâté*).
Lox	*Smoked salmon* Bagels and lox, that is, sliced bagels spread with cream cheese and covered with lox, are very popular in the US. *Smoked salmon* is available in most English supermarkets, and many fishmongers sell it as well.
Lunch	*Lunch*, *luncheon*, or *dinner* If the main meal of the day is eaten mid-day, then it is called *dinner*. Otherwise the mid-day meal is called *lunch* (or, less often, *luncheon*).
Macaroni & cheese	*Macaroni cheese*
Manicotti	Use *cannelloni* Manicotti, like cannelloni, is a tubular pasta which is usually filled with a meat or vegetable stuffing and then baked.
Marshmallow fluff	Marshmallow fluff is available in some supermarkets and may be used as a substitute for marshmallows in some recipes, but with varying results.

Marshmallows	When American recipes call for marshmallows, they mean the plain white ones and although these are available in English supermarkets, they never seem to be in stock when you need them (often resulting in trips to 2 or 3 supermarkets before finding them). They are stocked in the sweets aisle but may also be stocked in the baking section. A word of caution: be sure the bag you pick up contains only the plain white marshmallows as the ones most commonly stocked in England are the coloured, flavoured ones, or a mixture of the two. Plain white marshmallows are also available in speciality food shops. For addresses, see the *Mail Order and Shopping Guide* section.
Martini	In England, a martini can refer to the gin and vermouth cocktail but more often it refers to a drink consisting solely of vermouth, so it's best to state which type of martini you want. To make an American martini, combine two parts gin to one part dry vermouth (typically 1½ oz. gin to ¾ oz. vermouth), add ice and stir to cool it, then strain it into a cocktail glass. Serve with an olive or a twist of lemon.
Masa harina	Masa harina is a type of cornmeal which is ground in a special way and then treated with lime water. It's used for making corn tortillas and, in *The Moosewood Cookbook*, Mollie Katzen cautions against substituting with regular cornmeal. As of this writing, masa harina is available from both Lupe Pintos & Made in America (see the *Mail Order and*

Shopping Guide section). Otherwise, you'll have to make do with cornmeal.

Matzo or matzo meal   Matzo is square, unleavened, wheat crackers; matzo meal is finely ground matzo. Both are available in England from Jewish delis and butchers. (See *Jewish food*, this section.)

Measuring cup   *Measuring jug* or *measuring glass*

Measuring spoons   The measuring spoon sets sold in England typically include ½ teaspoon; 1 teaspoon (*5 ml*); dessertspoon (*10 ml*); and tablespoon (*15 ml*). Measuring spoon sets sold in America include ¼ teaspoon (but not dessertspoon).

Meat grinder   *Hand operated mincer*

Melon, honeydew   The honeydew sold in England (called *large yellow honeydew melon*) has a brilliant yellow skin, a mild flavour and is not as sweet as the smooth, pale-green skinned honeydew that is common throughout the US. Whereas the pale-green skinned honeydew is not normally available in England; the yellow-skinned honeydew is occasionally available in the US (though I have only come across it there once) and it is also called 'honeydew' there.

Mimosa   *Buck's fizz*
This is an alcoholic drink consisting of two parts champagne to one part orange juice.

Milk Chart   *See page 118.*

Milk, 1%   *See Milk, Lowfat entry.*

This page: the pale-green smooth-skinned honeydew sold in the US.
Next page: the brilliant-yellow honeydew melon sold in England.

Milk, 2%   *See Milk, Lowfat entry.*

Milk, condensed   Sweetened condensed milk is a mixture of milk
                           and sugar[6] which is heated until more than half
                           the water has evaporated. In England, the
                           average fat content of sweetened condensed
                           milk ranges from 0.2% for the skimmed to
                           10.1% for the whole milk kind. Note: In the
                           US, unsweetened condensed milk is called
                           evaporated milk but in England, there's a
                           difference between the way condensed milk and
                           evaporated milk are made[7] so here there's a
                           separate product called *unsweetened condensed*

---

[6]40-45% of the mixture is cane sugar.

[7]In England, condensed milk is milk which is pasteurized; evaporated milk
is not.

milk (made from whole milk and having a fat content between 7.5-15%).

Milk, Dry or Powdered	*Dried milk, powdered milk,* or *dehydrated milk* Dried milk is milk which has had its water removed. The most commonly available in both the US and Britain is made from skimmed milk, though dried milk made from whole milk is available.[8] To reconstitute dried milk, put 2 ounces of dried milk in a 20 ounce jug, fill with cold water, and stir.

Milk, Evaporated — American evaporated milk is milk which has had 60% of its water removed; British evaporated milk is milk which has been evaporated to half its original volume, then homogenized, canned, and sterilized, in that order. In the US, evaporated whole milk must contain at least 7.9% milkfat; in Britain, the same milk must contain at least 9% fat but no more than 15% (its average fat content is 9.4%). British evaporated partly-skimmed milk has an average fat content of 4%.

Milk, Lowfat — *Semi-skimmed milk,* also *half-fat milk*
Whereas the fat content of American lowfat milk ranges from 0.5% to 2%, fat in British *semi-skimmed milk* is between 1.5-1.8% (1.6% being the average fat content). Two common types of lowfat milk sold in the US are 2% milk and 1% milk (containing 2% and 1% milkfat, respectively).

---

[8]Due to its fat content, dry whole milk must be refrigerated.

Milk, Skim   *Skimmed milk*
and Nonfat   American skim milk (also called nonfat milk)
                    must, by law, contain less than 0.5% fat.
                    British *skimmed milk* must contain no more
                    than 0.3% fat (its average fat content is 0.1%).

Milk, Ultrapasteurized *UHT milk* or *long life milk*
                    UHT milk is milk that's been quickly heated to
                    above 132°C (270°F), held there for a few
                    seconds, and then rapidly cooled and packed in
                    sterile containers (usually boxes). Unopened, it
                    will keep for up to 6 months but once opened,
                    behaves like normal milk (i.e., needs
                    refrigeration and must be consumed within a
                    few days). *UHT milk* is much more prevalent
                    in England than ultrapasteurized milk is in the
                    US -- the miniature containers of milk that are
                    served with tea and coffee in England are
                    usually *UHT milk.*

Milk, Whole   *Whole milk,* also *full cream milk*
                    American whole milk must contain at least
                    3.5% milkfat (though this amount may vary
                    from state to state). British whole milk must
                    contain between 3.5% to 4.2% milkfat (its
                    average fat content is 3.8-3.9%). Although by
                    definition *full cream milk* refers to Channel
                    Islands milk, people and manufacturers loosely
                    use it to refer to any whole milk. Channel
                    Islands milk comes from Jersey or Guernsey
                    cows, small animals which produce a very rich
                    milk -- one with an average fat content of
                    between 4.8% and 5.1% (by law Channel
                    Islands milk must contain no less than 4% fat).
                    This type of milk is usually sold as 'breakfast
                    milk' in supermarkets.

Miracle Whip	*Salad cream* Miracle Whip is the name brand of a *salad cream* sold in the US; its brand name is often used interchangeably with the product name so occasionally you come across recipes calling for ½ cup of Miracle Whip.
Mirin	Mirin is a sweet cooking wine made from sake, sweet rice, and rice malt, and is used in many Japanese recipes. In England, you can find it in the larger Oriental stores, in select Sainsburys, and in some Asian shops but all these seem to be limited to the larger cities (e.g., London, Birmingham, Nottingham). (See *Addendum*, page 227.)
Molasses	Contrary to what you may have read, molasses is *not* the same as treacle. Molasses is sweeter, lighter in colour (more a dark brown than a brownish-black), less viscous, and not as bitter as treacle. Molasses is available in speciality food shops, some health food shops, but only occasionally in supermarkets. If you cannot locate any in your area, Martha Lomask suggests in *The All-American Cookbook* using equal parts of golden syrup and treacle instead. Although some food books say treacle is sweeter than molasses, this is only true as regards blackstrap molasses, and blackstrap is not the type of molasses Americans normally use in cooking. There are three types of molasses produced when sugar is refined: light, dark, and blackstrap. Light molasses is the mildest and sweetest of the three, and is used on pancakes and waffles. Dark molasses is the one most commonly used in American cooking (it's

the one used in gingerbread, shoofly pie, Boston
baked beans, etc.); it has a stronger flavour
than light molasses and is not as sweet.
Blackstrap molasses is very dark and thick,
with bitter overtones and almost no sweetness.
Although this is occasionally sold in health food
stores in the US, rarely is it used in cooking --
more commonly it is used in animal feed or
industrial alcohol.

Muffins	*American muffins* or simply *muffins* As of this writing, American muffins are available in many of the larger supermarkets. In the US they are usually eaten with breakfast; popular varieties include blueberry, bran, and corn muffins. Basic muffins are made with flour, eggs, milk, butter, baking powder and a little sugar.
Muffins, English	English muffins (called simply *muffins* in England) are similar in look to crumpets but are less moist. They are available in most supermarkets here.
Muffin pan or muffin tin	Muffin pans hold either six or twelve 2¾" (*7cm*) muffins; each cup holds 3½ to 4 ounces of batter. Muffin tins may be used for cupcakes as well as for muffins and are available in cookery shops. Alternatively you may use a deep patty pan.
Muscats	These are raisins made from Muscat (*muscatel*) grapes.
Napkins, table	*Serviettes* *Serviettes* are not widely used in British homes

(understatement). And in the service sector
they are often not provided (many ice cream
vendors in the summer don't even carry them).

Noodles, broad or wide	*See Broad noodles.*
Noodles, egg	*Tagliatelle*
Nuts	*Nuts* or *kernels*
Oats	*Oats* (in Scotland, *corn* - see Corn entry)
Oil, corn	*Corn oil* or *maize oil*
Oil, peanut	*Groundnut oil* or *peanut oil*
Oil, salad	Salad oil is any vegetable oil suitable for use in dressing salads (e.g., corn oil, sunflower oil).
Okra	*Okra* or *ladies fingers* Okra is available fresh in many supermarkets.
Oleo or oleomargarine	*Margarine* Margarine (originally called *oléomargarine*) was developed in France in the 1860s for a contest to find a substitute for butter. The word *oléo* is French for oil and the word 'margarine' stems from the French *margarique* (referring to margaric acid). I remember hearing the terms oleo and oleomargarine when I was a kid in the US, but wasn't sure whether these terms are used today so I wrote my Aunt Dee and here's what she said: *What is now called margarine used to be called oleo. Oleo came in a sealed plastic bag*

*in a square box. The contents looked like lard
(white). Inside the plastic bag was a little red
plastic capsule that you squeezed, breaking so
the color ran free and then you worked it into
the 'lard' (doing so through the plastic bag)
until it was evenly distributed to make a yellow
color like butter. I remember it well because
that was always my job when I was growing
up.[9] I used to hate it and am so glad you can
buy margarine in the form it is today.
Whenever I buy stick margarine which is in the
same kind of box the 'oleo' used to be in, I'm
always afraid when I open it up there will be a
plastic bag that has to be squeezed!*

Olives, ripe	*Black olives*

Orange juice   Juices are sold in boxes (and less commonly,
bottles or small tins) on the shelves, and also in
cartons in the refrigerated section. (See
Addendum, page 227.) In addition, *high-juice
squash* (which is a concentrate containing
approximately 40% juice) is available in the
soft drinks section of the supermarket. (NB:
Many brands of squash contain artificial
sweeteners.)

Organ meat   *Offal*
(e.g., kidneys; heart; liver; etc.)

Oven mitts   *Oven gloves*, occasionally *oven mitts*
An American oven mitt is typically a quilted,
heat-proof mitt worn to protect the hands when
handling hot pots and utensils. British *oven*

---

[9]This was in the 1940s.

gloves are similar to American oven mitts. However, *double oven gloves* are not. These refer to a long rectangular piece of thick fabric with a pocket at each end; you slip a hand in each pocket to protect them when retrieving hot pots from the oven.

Oyster
Oysters sold in Britain include 'natives' (*Ostrea edulis*); Portuguese or 'Ports' (*Crassotrea angulata*); and the type you're most likely so see in shops, the introduced giant Pacific oyster or 'gigas' (*Crassotrea gigas*). 'Natives' retain their eggs in the shell until fertilisation, which makes them unpleasant to eat during the breeding season (May-August), but 'Ports' and 'gigas' do not, so they may be eaten anytime.

Oyster cracker
Oyster crackers are tiny (¾" diameter [*19mm*]), puffy, round crackers traditionally served with oyster stew and other seafood chowders. As of this writing, they are not sold in England.

Pan
Tin
Baking pans, cake pans, etc. are usually called baking tins and cake tins. A bread pan is called a loaf tin.

Pancake
An American pancake is like a thick crêpe (~³/₁₆" [*5mm*] thick). British pancakes are the same as crêpes.

Pan-broil
Pan-broiling is a method of cooking meat in a frying pan *without* added fat. To pan-broil, you cook the meat slowly over a low heat and, as the fat from the meat melts, pour it off. Any

meat cut suitable for broiling is also suitable for pan-broiling.

Pan-fry

Fry
When an American recipe says to pan-fry something, it means to fry it in a frying pan, using a small amount of fat or oil. The term pan-frying is used to differentiate from deep-fat frying.

Papaya

Pawpaw or *papaya*
In England, papayas are called both *papayas* and *pawpaws*. However, pawpaw (or papaw) also exists as a different fruit entirely and is a member of the custard apple family. In Britain, *pawpaw* usually refers to a papaya.

Paper towels

Kitchen towels or *absorbent kitchen paper*

Partridge

Quail or *grouse*
No true partridge is native to North America, although the name 'partridge' is used: in northern US it refers to *ruffed grouse*; in the south it means *quail*.

Pasta, Bows

Farfalle

Pasta, Shells

Conchiglie

Patty pan (cymling)

Custard squash

Peanut Butter Cups

When I began this book, Reese's Peanut Butter Cups were available only in speciality food shops. As of this writing, Woolworths carry them. Peanut Butter Cups are a chocolate confection consisting of a peanut butter centre completely coated in thick milk chocolate. If you can't locate them here, you can make your own; for the recipe, see page 200.

Pears, Bartlett	*Williams pears*
Peas, black-eyed	*Black-eyed beans* *Black-eyed beans* are available in many health food shops and some supermarkets.
Pepper shaker	*Pepper pot*
Peppers, bell (also green, sweet or globe)	*Capsicum peppers* or *sweet peppers*
Periwinkles	*Winkles*
Piccalilli	Whereas English *piccalilli* is a bright yellow, coarse flavoured pickle made with dry mustard and having little or no sugar, American piccalilli often contains mustard seeds rather than dry mustard, and is usually made with more sugar than vinegar. English *piccalilli*, though less sweet, is closer to what Americans call mustard pickle or chow chow, than it is to American piccalilli.
Pickles, half-sour	Half-sour pickles are bright green and crunchy and often flavoured with garlic. They are available in some Jewish delis and kosher butchers, as well as in some speciality food shops. (See *Jewish foods*, this section.)
Pie dough	*Shortcrust pastry*
Pie plate	American pie plates usually have an 8 or 9" (*20-23 cm*) diameter and a narrow, flat rim. They are deeper (1-1½" [*2.5-4 cm*]) than the

shallow, wide-rimmed British pie plates. If you don't mind the fluted edges, you may use a flan tin or flan dish instead.

Pie shell or pie crust   *Pastry case*

Pig in a blanket   This is a fast food made by deep-frying a batter-dipped hot dog. The difference between this and corn dogs is the batter: corn dogs are dipped in a cornmeal batter.

Pit (e.g., cherry pit)   *Stone*

Plastic wrap   *Cling film*

Popcorn   The name is the same but more often than not it is prepared 'sweet' in England. This is a warning so that you don't find yourself in a darkened cinema thinking someone spilled sugar in your popcorn. If what you want is regular buttered popcorn, you may need to pop it at home. (See instructions on page 203.) Popcorn kernels are available in plastic bags from many health food shops and also from dried fruit and nut stalls. Microwave popcorn is available from some supermarkets, as is popcorn already-popped (but, already-popped popcorn is often the sweetened kind).

Popovers   Popovers are essentially the same as Yorkshire pudding. They are baked in custard cups or deep muffin tins.

Popsicles   *Ice lollies*
Ice lollies sold in the UK often contain an artificial sweetener.

PORK CUTS

In the US, fresh pork cuts come from the same hogs or pigs as bacon, ham, and other cured and/or smoked cuts. In England, bacon, gammon, and ham come from pigs specially reared to produce a certain proportion of lean meat to fat. Incidentally, in the US, we do not have a cut of meat called gammon, and since the difference between gammon and ham causes much confusion, I will explain. Both gammon and ham are the hind leg of the pig but to produce ham, the hind leg is cut from the pig and then cured separately (according to local methods); for gammon, a 'bacon pig' is cured in brine *before* the gammon is cut from the pig. Also, gammon is cut square at the top while ham is cut round. Both gammon and ham may be either smoked or unsmoked. And a cooked gammon is often described as ham. *Now* do you understand? Oh yes, and Americans call the leg of the pig 'ham' whether it's cured or not -- if it's not cured, they call it 'fresh ham' (a bit of a contradiction if you ask me, but there you go).

Pork is a very popular meat in the US and as such, there are any number of cuts (and names for these cuts). American pork cuts often differ somewhat from the English cuts so I have not always tried to give equivalents. What I have done is to list the names and descriptions of the various American cuts, including the section of the animal the particular cut is from, plus the appropriate cooking methods for that cut. (Bear in mind that although an English cut might have the same name as an American cut, they might not be the same cut, so go primarily by the description -- especially the section of the animal the cut is from -- rather than its American name.) Also, since American butchers and British butchers cut up a pig differently, I have included illustrations to show you the differences. This should help you or your butcher to select a roughly equivalent British cut.

NOTE: Bear in mind that although the BRITISH PORK CUTS diagram that follows is, for the most part, correct for England, there are regional differences, as well as differences between the way a Scottish and

PORK CUTS, *cont.*

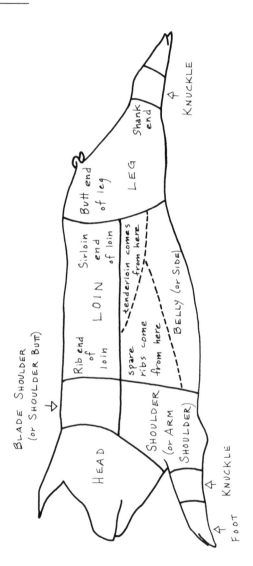

AMERICAN PORK CUTS

PORK CUTS, *cont.*

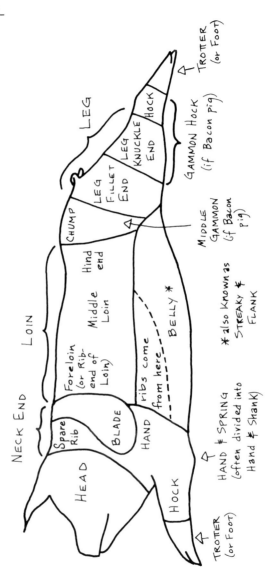

BRITISH PORK CUTS

PORK CUTS, *cont.*

English pig is cut up. The *hand & spring* section (comprised of the lower shoulder [the hand], the jowl, knuckle, trotter, and first 3 or 4 bones of the belly) is, in northeast England, called *shoulder*, and in Scotland, called a *runner*. (Also, in Scotland, the *knuckle* is called a *hough*.) The *neck end* (i.e., the upper part of the shoulder consisting of the *spare rib* and *blade*) is, in northeast England, called a *chine* and in Scotland called *shoulder*. (Also, the Scottish *shoulder* is cut larger and may weigh as much as 20 lbs.) And, as in lamb, the leg of the animal is, in Scotland, called *gigot*.

Some common American cuts of pork are listed below.

Arm roast
: This cut, also known as shoulder arm roast, is from the lower portion of the shoulder (*hand and spring*) section and has the shank removed. It contains a small round bone, and is suitable for roasting.

Arm steak
: This slightly oval steak is cut from the arm roast and contains a small round (arm) bone. It is suitable for braising and frying.

Back ribs
: Back ribs are from the loin section near the shoulder blade and have very little meat on them. They are suitable for roasting, broiling (*grilling*), braising, and cooking in liquid.

Boston butt roast
: *See Shoulder blade roast.*

Bulk pork sausage
: *Sausage meat*
Bulk pork sausage refers to the meat mixture that's used to fill sausage casings. If you have a recipe that calls for this, ask your butcher for *sausage meat* and they'll know what you mean.

PORK CUTS, *cont.*

Butterfly chops	A butterfly chop is made from a boneless chop from the loin section. To make a butterfly chop, cut a boneless pork chop almost in half (so that it's half as thick as it was), and spread each side out flat so that its shape resembles a butterfly. Since this technique exposes twice the surface area of the meat, it cooks more quickly than a regular boneless chop. These chops are suitable for broiling (*grilling*), pan-broiling, frying, and braising.
Country-style ribs	Country-style or country ribs are from the loin section and contain either rib bones or backbones. These meaty ribs are suitable for braising, broiling (*grilling*), roasting, or cooking in liquid.
Fatback	*Back fat*
	Back fat is the more appropriate name for that is exactly what this is: it's the layer of plain white fat that runs along the pig's back. *Back fat* is fresh (as opposed to cured, salted, or smoked) and is sold for larding meat; for barding; and for lining molds for pâtés.
Fresh ham slice or center slice	This oval-shaped cut is from the hind leg of the animal and contains a small round bone and 4 separate muscles. It is suitable for broiling (*grilling*) and roasting.
Head cheese	*Brawn*
	Head cheese (or *brawn*) is a highly gelatinous compressed mixture of bits and pieces of meat

PORK CUTS, *cont.*

from the pig's head. In the US, it is sold as cold cuts.

Loin blade roast

This roast goes by any number of names in the US, including 5-rib roast, 7-rib roast and rib end roast. It is cut from the shoulder end of the loin section and contains a portion of the blade and rib bones.

Loin center rib roast

This roast, also known in the US as center cut pork roast, is from the centre of the loin. It contains loin eye muscle and rib bones and is rather expensive.

Loin chops

Pork loin chops or loin end chops are from the loin section and contain loin and tenderloin muscles, usually with a T-shaped bone separating the muscles. They are suitable for braising and frying.

Loin rib chops

In the US, these are also known as center cut pork chops or rib chops, and are smaller and less choice than the chops known simply as loin chops. They are cut from the rib end of the loin and contain rib bone but no tenderloin. They are suitable for just about everything: roasting, broiling (*grilling*), frying; and braising.

Loin sirloin chops

These chops (also known as sirloin pork chops) are from the sirloin end (or *hind end*) of the loin and contain a bone. They are suitable for braising, broiling (*grilling*), and frying. *Chump chops* would make a suitable substitute.

PORK CUTS, *cont.*

Loin sirloin cutlets	These boneless tender slices cut from the sirloin end (or *hind end*) of the loin are suitable for braising, broiling (*grilling*), and frying. *Noisettes* or *boneless chump chops* would make suitable substitutes.
Picnic	*See Shoulder arm picnic.*
Pig's feet	*Trotters* Pig's feet may be either cut short (4-6" [*10-15cm*]) or cut long, to include the hock. (Chinese and Italian markets cut them long.) They are suitable for braising and cooking in liquid.
Pork hocks	Pork hocks are cut from the 'picnic shoulder', which is from the shoulder (*hand and spring*) section. The hock is the 2-3" (*5-7.5cm*) piece that's removed from the end of the picnic shoulder when it is cut short. They are round, tapering, skin-covered pieces containing shank bones and some very edible meat, and are suitable for braising and cooking in liquid.
Pork leg, whole	The leg is also referred to as a 'fresh' ham (as opposed to a cured ham). This cut contains the hind leg bone and is suitable for roasting.
Pork sausage	The minced pork used in American pork sausage is normally from the blade shoulder section. When the minced pork is mixed with seasonings, it's referred to as bulk pork sausage (*cf* Bulk pork sausage); when the bulk pork sausage is packed into casings, then it becomes pork sausage. American pork sausage may or

PORK CUTS, *cont.*

	may not be smoked. It is suitable for frying, braising, and baking.
Rib crown roast	To get a rib crown roast, you fasten together two loin roasts in the shape of a crown.
Rolled Boston butt	*See Shoulder blade roast, boneless.*
Shoulder arm picnic	The picnic shoulder or picnic is from the shoulder (*hand and spring*) section and contains the forearm and shank.[10] It is cut deep into the shoulder and around and down to the front foot, in the shape of a small ham, and is suitable for roasting.
Shoulder blade roast	This roast, also known in the US as Boston butt and pork butt, is from the upper shoulder (*blade*) and contains a portion of the blade bone.
Shoulder blade roast, boneless	This roast (also known as boneless blade roast and rolled Boston butt) is the shoulder blade roast boned, rolled, and tied. (See Shoulder blade roast.)
Shoulder blade steak	This steak, also known as blade steak, is cut from the shoulder blade roast and is suitable for braising, broiling (*grilling*), or frying. (See Shoulder blade roast.)
Sirloin roast	A sirloin roast is a roast cut from the sirloin end (*hind end*) of the loin.

---

[10]The shank section is that nearest the knuckle.

PORK CUTS, *cont.*

Spareribs

Spare ribs
Not to be confused with the *spare rib joint* of an English pig -- that is near the head, and cuts from it are called *spare rib chops*; these spareribs are from the belly section and are long rib bones with a very thin covering of meat. They are suitable for roasting, broiling (*grilling*), braising, and cooking in liquid.

Tenderloin

Fillet
The tenderloin (or *fillet*) is the lean, tender muscle that lies beneath the backbone at the sirloin end (*hind end*) of the loin. It is suitable for roasting, braising, broiling (*grilling*), or frying.

CURED CUTS:

Bacon

Rindless unsmoked streaky bacon and *Danish plain (or unsmoked) streaky rindless bacon*, are similar to American-style bacon. American bacon comes from the belly[11] of the pig and is cured and smoked. It is saltier and yields more fat than English bacon, and whereas the sliced bacon sold in the US is rindless; *bacon rashers* (i.e., slices of bacon) sold here come with or without a rind so you may need to trim the rind. (To cook bacon for BLTs, see the Bacon entry on page 4.)

---

[11]In England, the belly of the pig is also known as *streaky*, hence *streaky bacon*.

PORK CUTS, *cont.*

CURED CUTS, *cont.*

Canadian bacon	Canadian-style bacon is made from the loin muscle of the pig which is rolled and cured and then sold in large pieces or in slices. It is more like ham than bacon in both taste and appearance and is suitable for roasting, broiling (*grilling*), and frying. In Canada, it is called back bacon. A *gammon steak* would make a reasonable substitute.
Ham, country	Country hams are hams which are more heavily cured and smoked than the ready-to-eat hams sold in the supermarkets in the US, and they are much tastier. Before boiling or baking, they need to be soaked first. (A well-known American country ham is Smithfield ham, a specially cured ham from Smithfield, Virginia.)
Prosciutto	If you're looking for prosciutto (which is actually just Italian for 'ham'), use *Parma ham* or *Spanish Serrano ham* (currently available in Sainsburys). *Parma ham*, which is a seasoned, salt-cured, and air-dried (not smoked) ham, reputedly has a less pronounced flavour than *Serrano ham*, but I couldn't detect a difference (not between the two packaged supermarket products, anyway). With melon, either of these hams makes a very nice (if dear) *starter*.
Salt pork	Salt pork is used as a flavouring in certain American dishes, such as Boston baked beans. It is primarily fat, with some streaks of lean, and comes from the part of the pig known as

PORK CUTS, *cont.*

CURED CUTS, *cont.*

the side pork or siding (below the loin and extending through the centre of the pig). The side pork is used for both bacon and salt pork: for bacon, it's smoked; for salt pork, it's salted.

Smoked ham center slice
This is the ham slice or center slice, smoked. It comes either with the round arm bone or boneless, and ranges from ½"-2" thick. It is suitable for broiling (*grilling*) and roasting.

Smoked ham rump portion (or butt half)
The smoked ham rump portion is cut from the upper portion or butt half of the ham (minus several center slices), and is suitable for roasting.

Smoked ham shank portion
The smoked ham shank portion is cut from the lower portion or shank half of the ham (minus several center slices), and is usually less expensive than the upper portion which is called the butt half. It is suitable for roasting.

Smoked pork shoulder picnic
A smoked picnic (also known as picnic ham and smoked callie) is essentially a ham made from the *front* leg of the pig rather than the back leg. It is suitable for roasting or cooking in liquid.

Smoked whole ham
This is a cured and smoked whole pork leg and may weigh from 12-14 pounds. It is suitable for roasting.

Pot

Pan
In America, a pot is a fairly deep cooking vessel with a handle whereas a pan in America normally refers to a shallow, wide, open container, usually of metal and without a lid (the exception being a saucepan). However, in England a *pan* is virtually any cooking vessel used on the stovetop while a *pot* is a rounded container, often of earthenware, for holding liquids or solids -- more along the lines of an American casserole dish. In many areas of England, people speak of *doing the pots* rather than washing the dishes. *Pots* in England also refers to what Americans call tubs, for example, a *pot* of yogurt rather than a tub of yogurt.

Potato, sweet

There are two types of sweet potato: a dry one with pinkish-yellow flesh which is cooked and eaten like a regular potato, and a sweeter, softer, bright orange variety which is usually baked in a casserole. Sweet potatoes are available in England from some supermarkets and speciality food shops but both varieties are not always available at the same time. (At this writing, the orange sweet potato is available from Safeway but not the other variety; in the past, the reverse was true.)

Potato chips

Crisps or *potato crisps.*

Potholders

American potholders normally refer to squares of quilted fabric, typically 7" (*18 cm*) square, and used for protecting the hands when handling hot pots or utensils. They also can refer to oven mitts (*oven gloves*).

Pretzel	Pretzels are an ancient food which originated in Roman times and migrated to the US sometime in the 1600s (probably via the Dutch). Today pretzels are available in the US in one of two forms: bread-like & chewy, or crisp & cracker-like. Crisp pretzels come in the form of sticks ('thins'), circles ('rings'), or a loose knot (like the Staffordshire knot) and are available in some British supermarkets. The large, soft & chewy, knot-shaped pretzels (like the ones sold by street vendors in Philadelphia and New York) are not currently available in England.
Proof (of alcohol)	'Proof' is the term used to show the absolute alcohol content of distilled liquors and can be related to weight or to volume, depending upon the country. In America, the proof of a liquor is twice the percent of that alcohol, e.g., a vodka that is 50% alcohol by volume will be 100 proof. British proof is (as you might've guessed) arrived at through a number of complicated calculations but roughly speaking, it is 57% alcohol by volume. To convert US proof to UK proof, multiply by 7 and divide by 8; to convert UK proof to US proof, multiply by 8 and divide by 7.*
Proof yeast (*v*)	In breadmaking, proofing yeast means testing the yeast to ensure it is still active. To proof yeast, add one package (1 tablespoon) of *dried yeast* to ½ cup (4 oz./*120ml*) of warm water, add around one tablespoon (*15ml*) of sugar (or honey), stir it and set it aside for about 5

---

* Thanks to Tom Stobart's *The Cook's Encyclopaedia* for the calculations.

minutes. If the yeast is still active, this mixture will swell and bubbles will appear on top.

Prosciutto

use *Parma ham* or *Spanish Serrano ham*

Pumpernickel

Pumpernickel bread is available in some speciality food shops and occasionally in some supermarkets. (To make your own, see the recipe on page 149.)

Pumpkin, canned

Tinned pumpkin
Canned pumpkin is sometimes a mixture of pumpkin and winter squash, rather than all pumpkin. It is available in many speciality food shops and occasionally is available in supermarkets (I saw it once in Sainsburys). If you can't find it, you can grow the pumpkins yourself or buy them in the autumn (if you can find them), and make a puree from them. For instructions on how to make the puree, see page 215.

Punch down

Knock back
See *Dough, yeast*

Quahog

See *Clams*, this section.

Quiche

Savoury flan or quiche

Quiche pan

Flan dish

Raisins, black

Raisins
Raisins sold in the US are seedless; raisins sold in England include seedless California raisins as well as the highly regarded muscatel varieties, which contain pips. If the pips put you off, then buy the less-sweet California ones instead.

FOOD NAMES *Page 93*

Raisins, golden or
white

Sultanas

Rise (*v*)
(let dough rise)

Rise, or if it's the second rising, *prove.*
(let dough *prove*)
(See *Dough, yeast*, this section.)

Roast (*n*)

Joint
Americans often refer to a roast beef as simply
'a roast', just as the English often refer to a
roast joint of meat as 'a joint'.

Root beer

Root beer is available in speciality food shops
but is not normally found in supermarkets.
However, sarsaparilla is similar to root beer
and is available in the north of England (but
usually contains an artificial sweetener). If you
wish to make your own sarsaparilla, Walsh's in
Blackburn make an 'Extract for Making
Sarsaparilla Beer'. (See *Mail Order &
Shopping Guide* section.)

Rutabaga

Swede (or, esp. Scotland, *turnip*)
A rutabaga or *swede* is a pale yellow root
vegetable, resembling a large turnip (3-5"
diameter) but, unlike the turnip, is smooth right
up to its base. 'Rutabaga' is from the Swedish
rotabagge, hence '*swede*'.

Rye bread

When I began this book in the early 1990s, rye
bread was only available in England from
Jewish delis and some speciality and health food
shops. Lately, however, it's appeared in
supermarkets and even at the baker's stall in
Burton market. (To make your own rye bread,
see the recipe on page 153.)

Rye flour   Rye flour is available in some health food shops
                      and supermarkets.

Saccharin   The use of saccharin in the US is normally
                      restricted to dietetic products, labelled 'diet' or
                      'low-cal'. In England, saccharin is used in one
                      of two ways: either as an inexpensive
                      substitute for sugar[12] or as a low-calorie
                      substitute. When used as an inexpensive sugar-
                      substitute, the food and drink containing it will
                      have no special labelling; when used as a low-
                      calorie sugar-substitute, the food and drink
                      containing it will be labelled 'low-calorie' or
                      'diet'. The amount of saccharin used in British
                      soft drinks is restricted, and it is not permitted
                      at all in ice cream (although it is permitted in
                      ice lollies and other water-based frozen
                      confections).

Sage, dried or ground *Rubbed sage*
                      Rubbed sage is fluffier than ground sage but
                      the two may be used interchangeably.

Salad oil   See *Oil, salad*, this section.

Salt, kosher   Kosher salt is available from Jewish delis (see
                      Jewish foods entry) and some supermarkets
                      (but in much smaller containers than the 3 lb.
                      boxes sold in the US). Although water is
                      involved in the processing of kosher salt,[13] the
                      salt itself is from underground salt deposits -- it

---

[12] The widespread use of artificial sweeteners began in England during
WWII, when sugar was rationed.

[13] This applies to the production of Diamond Crystal kosher salt; I don't
know whether all kosher salt is made this way.

is not sea salt. Kosher salt has a jagged texture and is pure salt with no additives. It's less salty-tasting than regular table salt and is preferred by many famous cooks (e.g., James Beard; Madhur Jaffrey; Julie Sahni). One teaspoon of table salt equals about 1¾ teaspoons of kosher salt.

Salt pork	Salt pork is salted pork fat that's used as a flavouring in certain American dishes, such as Boston baked beans. (For further details, see Salt Pork in the Pork Cuts section on page 88.)
Salt shaker	*Salt cellar* (or, less commonly, *salt shaker*)
Sandwich, chicken salad	A chicken salad sandwich in England means a sandwich made with chicken meat and salad ingredients (e.g., cress; cucumber; tomato). The sandwich Americans understand as chicken salad (i.e., with a filling of chopped chicken, celery and walnuts, in a mayonnaise base), I've not seen in England. To make an American *chicken salad sandwich*, see the recipe on page 145.
Sausage, bulk pork	*Sausage meat* For more information, see the Bulk pork sausage entry in the Pork section on page 82.
Scallions	*Spring onions* or *salad onions*
Scampi	*Scampi* or *Dublin Bay prawn* Scampi are about 4" (*10cm*) long and unlike other prawns, have claws.
Scotch	*Whisky* In England, *whisky* refers to scotch whisky. If

you want a different type of whisky, you must specify the type.

Sell by date

Display until date
Products must be sold prior to their 'sell by' or *Display until* date, and should be consumed before their *Best before end* or *BBE* date.

Seltzer

Fizzy water or *sparkling water* or *carbonated water*

Sheet cake

See *Cake, sheet* this section.

Sherbet

Sorbet is very similar to US sherbet. In England, *sherbet* often refers to a powdered candy, similar to Lik 'm Ade in America.

Shortening

White sunflower vegetable fat, White Flora, and *Trex* are all similar to American shortening. Alternatively, you may use either *Cookeen* or *soft vegetable lard* (though contrary to what its name implies, it isn't very soft). 'Shortening' can mean any kind of fat or oil used in pastry making but in the US, it has come to mean a specific type of fat: a soft, white, vegetable fat (e.g., 'Crisco'). It is normally sold in round cardboard tubs and stocked with the dry baking goods while in England it is sold in 500g boxes and stocked in the refrigerated section of the supermarket.

Shrimp

Small shrimp are called *shrimp*; large shrimp are usually called *prawns* and very large 'shrimp' (about 4" [*10cm*]) with claws are called *scampi* or *Dublin Bay prawns. Shrimp* and *prawns* are usually sold already boiled, with or without their shells.

L-R: English White Flora, American Crisco, and English vegetable fat.

Shrimp, butterfly	*Prawn cutlet*
Skillet	*Frying pan* In England, *skillet* normally refers to a small metal pot with a long handle, and usually with legs. In America, skillet means simply a *frying pan*.
Snow peas	*Mange tout* (i.e., eat all)
Soda or soda pop	*Soft drink* or *fizzy drink*
Sour cream	See *Cream, sour* this section.
Sourdough	Sourdough breads are made using a different strain of yeast (*saccharomyces exiguus*) from that of other breads. Although you can make sourdough bread by allowing yeast to ferment

and then adding it to the flour mixture, it will not have quite the same flavour as San Francisco's sourdough bread.

Soy

Usually it's *soya* here (except for the sauce which, as in the US, is called *soy sauce*).

Spatula

Fish slice or *lifter*
In England, a metal spatula is often called a *fish slice* (for lifting fish cakes) or *lifter* while a plastic spatula (used for scraping bowls clean) is called a *spatula*.

Spoon, slotted

Straining spoon

Spring-form pan

See *Cake pans, spring-form*, this section.

Sprouts

There are all sorts of sprouts but in the US, if the type of sprout isn't specified (e.g., mung bean sprouts or simply, bean sprouts), then usually a sprouted seed, similar to *cress* or *salad cress* is meant.

Squash, spaghetti

Vegetable spaghetti

Squash, summer

Summer squash are distinguished by their thin, edible skins and soft, edible seeds. Varieties of summer squash include the yellow crookneck (or crooked) squash; straightneck (or yellow) squash; zucchini (*courgettes*) and golden zucchini (*yellow courgettes*); and patty pan (also called cymling and scalloped squash). Yellow squash (both crookneck and straightneck) are virtually unavailable in England. *Yellow courgettes* are only occasionally available in supermarkets, and some garden centres carry their seeds. (By the

*Seed packets of gold rush squash (yellow courgettes)
and yellow summer crookneck squash.*

way, if you were to ask in a supermarket if they
carry squash, you might be directed to the
drinks aisle. Squash here is more commonly
known as a concentrated liquid fruit drink.)

Steep (*verb*)

Mash, brew, or *steep*
Depending upon where you are in Britain, tea is
mashed, brewed, or, less commonly, *steeped.*

Stove

Cooker
The *cooker* is comprised of the *hob* (stovetop,
US), *grill* (broiler, US), and a main (and
sometimes secondary) oven. Most *Gas cookers*
are 'directly heated', creating zones of heat in
the oven so that only the middle shelf
corresponds to the temperature setting (the shelf

above will be one setting hotter, and the shelf
below one setting cooler). In England, *stove*
usually refers to an old-style gas stove.
American stoves are typically much larger than
English *cookers*. Below, I've compared my
sister's stove with my *cooker*.

	US	UK
width of stovetop[14] (*hob*):	29"	21"
inside width of oven:	24"	18"
inside height of oven:	17"	15½"

Stovetop   *Hob*

Strainer   *Metal sieve* or *strainer*

Submarine sandwich   *Baguette*
or hoagie or grinder   *Baguette* is both the name of the bread used as
                        well as the name of the prepared sandwich.
                        The prepared *baguette* sold in England won't
                        usually have the same types of fillings as an
                        American sub (e.g., meatball; pepper and egg;
                        sausage; salami) but you can always get a
                        baguette or *French stick* from the baker or
                        supermarket and prepare your own. (See also
                        Grinder entry on page 47).

Succotash   Originally called *misickquatash*, succotash was
                        a Narragansett Indian dish made of corn and
                        kidney beans and cooked in bear grease.
                        Today, succotash is made with corn and lima
                        beans and cooked with salt pork.

---

[14]On a typical English *hob*, the four burners adjoin one another while on a
typical American stovetop, there is a space running between the two rows of
burners. This space is usually about the width of a burner and it's a
convenient place to lay spoons, ingredients, etc. as you cook.

Sugar, brown	There are a variety of brown sugars sold in England, including *demerara, light golden soft sugar, rich dark soft sugar*, and *muscovado*. These all range in molasses content with *demerara* having the least at 1.5% and *muscovado* having the most (20%). For American recipes calling for dark brown sugar use *rich dark soft sugar*; for those calling for light brown sugar, use *light golden soft sugar*. (Safeway's *dark brown muscovado* and *light brown muscovado* may be substituted for dark brown sugar and light brown sugar, respectively.)
Sugar, confectioners or powdered	*Icing sugar* *Icing sugar* in the UK is mixed with calcium phosphate while confectioners or powdered sugar in the US is mixed with corn starch (*cornflour*).
Sugar, granulated	Use *granulated sugar* if available. Otherwise, substitute using *caster sugar* and adjust the amounts called for: the crystal size of *caster sugar* is approximately half that of granulated, so be sure to weigh it (rather than measure it in cups) to ensure equivalent amounts. Other forms of granulated sugars include *extra fine sugar*, used in drinks vending machines and in mixed alcoholic drinks, and *preserving sugar*, used in making jellies and jams. *Preserving sugar* has a crystal size more than twice that of *granulated sugar*.
Sugar, superfine	*Caster sugar* (Also see 'Sugar, granulated'.)
Sugar, turbinado	*Demerara sugar* (Also see 'Sugar, brown'.)

Supper	*Tea* or *dinner* (Also see 'Dinner' entry.) In England, *supper* refers to a late night meal eaten around or after 9pm. In many parts of the US, supper refers to the main meal of the day served around 6pm.
Swiss chard	*Swiss chard* or *seakale beet* If a recipe calls for Swiss chard and you cannot find it, use baby beet greens instead.
Taco	Tacos are a Mexican/American Indian food that gained popularity in the US through fast food chains like Taco Bell. A taco is made using a lightly fried (or baked) corn tortilla which is filled with a kidney bean (and/or minced meat) mixture and then topped with chopped lettuce and tomato, shredded cheese, and sour cream. Taco shells are available in British supermarkets.
Taffy	*Toffee* *Toffee* is called both 'taffy' and 'toffee' in the US.
Take-out food	*Take-away food*
Tamale	Tamales, originally an Aztec Indian food, are widely available throughout the US from Mexican restaurants and from the frozen food sections of the supermarket. A tamale (pron. tah-MAH-lay) is made using a cornmeal mixture which is spread onto a corn husk and topped with a savoury sauce. The corn husk is then wrapped around the mixture, and steamed. It yields a moist savoury corn cake.

Tea, hot	Tea in England is often served with milk already in it. If you want your tea black, be sure to say so before the tea is poured.
Tea, iced	The English do not, as a rule, drink iced tea. However, some supermarkets have started carrying cans of prepared iced tea, but this tea is often carbonated. To make iced tea, see the recipe on page 208.
Tomato paste	*Double concentrated tomato puree* This is available in both squeeze tubes and tins.
Tomato puree	*Creamed tomatoes* (See *Addendum*, p. 228.) American tomato puree is different from British (*double concentrated*) *tomato puree*. Whereas British *tomato puree* is the same as American tomato paste, American tomato puree is like a thick tomato sauce (American tomato sauce, that is -- not ketchup), and is made from tomatoes which have been briefly cooked and then strained. It is not currently available in England as 'tomato puree'.
Tomato sauce	*Passata, salsina* American tomato sauce is slightly thinner than American tomato puree and, as of this writing, is not sold in English supermarkets -- not as 'tomato sauce' anyway. There are, however, a number of other products sold here which are virtually indistinguishable from American tomato sauce (e.g., *passata, salsina*), and these may be used in its place. (NB In England, ketchup is often referred to as *tomato sauce*.) For seasoned tomato sauce, see the lasagne recipe on page 173.

Tortilla	A tortilla (pronounced tor-TEE-ah) is a flat, soft Mexican/American Indian bread made from ground cornmeal or (white) wheat flour. Tortillas are available from many British supermarkets.
Tostada	Tostadas, originally from Mexico and the Southwest, have become a popular American fast food. A tostada is made using a tortilla which is lightly fried, transferred to a plate, and covered with a bean and/or meat filling, and sprinkled with shredded cheese. This is then covered with a mound of chopped lettuce and tomato, and topped with a dollop of guacamole (pron. gua-ka-MOH-lay).
Tube pan	See Cake pans, tube, this section.
Turnip, French	*White-fleshed swedes*
Vanilla bean	*Vanilla pod*
Variety meats	*Offal* (e.g., kidneys; heart; liver; etc.)
Veal cuts	*See following page.*
Vegetables, raw	*Crudités* *Crudités* are raw vegetables (and/or fruit) cut up for dips. *Crudités* are sometimes sold in the produce sections of supermarkets.
Walnut, English	*Walnut* The American (or black) walnut is different from the English walnut but the two may be used interchangeably in recipes.

VEAL CUTS

American and British cuts of veal do not exactly correspond so to help you determine which part of the animal a particular cut is from, I have included illustrations showing how a British butcher cuts up a veal carcass and also how an American butcher cuts one up.

Some common American cuts of veal are listed below. Their descriptions include which section of the animal the cut is from, and also the appropriate cooking methods for the cut, so that should help you to select a roughly equivalent British cut of veal. If in doubt, describe the cut to your butcher for assistance.

Arm roast	Arm roast is cut from the shoulder and contains the arm bone (a round bone) and usually part of the rib bones. It is suitable for roasting or braising.
Arm steak	Arm steak is an oval-shaped steak cut from the shoulder and contains the arm bone and a rib bone. It is suitable for braising or frying.
Breast of veal	The veal breast is cut from the breast area under the rib section. It is a thin, flat cut containing the breast bone, lower ribs, and rib cartilage. It's quite lean, with some layering of fat, and is suitable for braising and roasting.
Breast riblets	Veal breast riblets (or veal riblets) are rectangular strips of meat made by cutting between the ribs. They're from the breast section and contain rib bones, and are suitable for braising or cooking in liquid.

VEAL CUTS, *cont.*

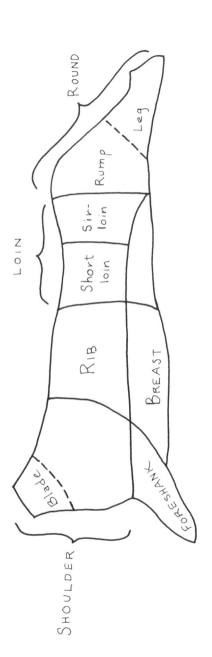

AMERICAN VEAL CUTS

VEAL CUTS, *cont.*

BRITISH VEAL CUTS

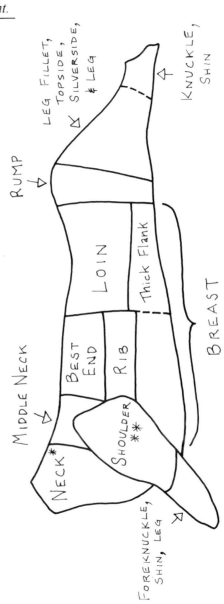

LEG FILLET, TOPSIDE, SILVERSIDE, & LEG

KNUCKLE, SHIN

RUMP

LOIN

Thick Flank

BREAST

MIDDLE NECK

BEST END

RIB

NECK*

SHOULDER **

FOREKNUCKLE, SHIN, LEG

* also known as SCRAG END.
** also known as CLOD.

VEAL CUTS, *cont.*

Breast roast, boneless	The boneless breast roast is the breast of veal boned, rolled, and tied. It is suitable for braising and roasting.
Crown roast	A crown roast is cut from the rib section (the *best end* section in England). The tips of the rib bones are trimmed of fat and lean, and then fastened to form a crown.
Cube steak	Veal cube steak is a mechanically tenderised cut from the shoulder, loin, or round (*leg fillet*) sections.
Cutlets, veal	*Escalopes* or *fillets* In the US, veal cutlets are thin, boneless slices from the leg section; in England, the cutlets come from the *best end* section and contain a bone (see Rib chop). American cutlets are usually ½-¾" (*12-19mm*) thick and are often pounded, especially in recipes calling for rolling or stuffing. They are usually braised or fried.
Leg rump roast	Veal leg rump roast (also known as veal rump roast or rump of veal) contains the leg bone and is from the rump section (or, in England, the *rump* and *leg fillet* sections). It is suitable for braising and roasting.
Leg rump roast, boneless	Boneless leg rump roast (also known as rolled rump roast or rump of veal, boneless) is the leg rump roast with the leg bone removed, and the roast rolled and tied. It comes from the rump section (or, in England, the *rump* and *leg*

VEAL CUTS, *cont.*

	fillet sections) and is suitable for braising and roasting.
Loin chops	Veal loin chops contain tenderloin and are similar to beef Porterhouse steaks in that they have a T-bone and a fair portion of lean meat. They are from the loin section and are suitable for braising or frying.
Loin roast	Veal loin roast is cut from the loin section and contains the T-bone. It is suitable for roasting and braising.
Ossi buchi or Osso buco	*Osso buco* As you might have guessed, this dish of braised veal is Italian in origin. *Osso buco* calls for slices of veal shank, 1½" thick, with bone and marrow. Veal shank is cut from the foreshank or *foreknuckle* section.
Rack	*Best end* A rack is a roast of rib chops. The section it is from is called the rib section in the US and the *best end* section in England.
Rib chop	*Cutlets* A rib chop contains a rib bone and rib eye muscle (but not the tenderloin) and should be braised, fried or broiled (*grilled*). The section it is from is called the rib section in the US and the *best end* section in England. NB When the term 'veal cutlet' is used in an American cookbook, it refers to a thin boneless cut from

VEAL CUTS, *cont.*

	the leg; in an English cookbook it refers to a bone-in cut from the *best end.*
Rib roast	*Best end* A rib roast has 2 or more ribs and includes the rib eye muscle, featherbones and part of the chine bone (i.e., the thick part where the rib joins the backbone). In the US, a rib roast is cut from the rib section; the equivalent English cut is from the *best end* section.
Rolled cutlets	See Scaloppine entry, below.
Scaloppine	*Very thin escalopes or fillets* Also known as veal scallops. Scaloppine are small, thin pieces of veal leg, pounded to $1/8$" to $1/16$" thick, and usually sautéed or braised. When they are rolled with a stuffing, tied and braised, they're known as veal birds or rolled cutlets; when they are deep-fried, they're wiener schnitzel.
Shank cross cut	This cut of meat is a cross cut from the foreshank section (called the *foreknuckle* section in England) and is suitable for braising or cooking in liquid.
Shoulder blade roast	*Shoulder roasting joint with blade bone* The shoulder blade roast is cut from the shoulder section and contains a portion of the blade bone. (The area it's cut from is called the *neck, middle neck,* and *shoulder* sections in England.)

VEAL CUTS, *cont.*

Shoulder blade steak

Shoulder blade steaks (also known as shoulder veal chops or veal blade steak) are cut from the shoulder blade roast, and are suitable for braising or frying. They are less expensive than veal rib chops or loin chops.

Shoulder roast, boneless

Shoulder roasting joint, boneless
The boneless shoulder roast is cut from the shoulder section, has the bones removed, and is rolled and tied. It is suitable for braising or roasting.

Shoulder steak, boneless

Shoulder roasting joint, boneless, cut up into steaks
Boneless shoulder steaks are steaks cut from the boneless shoulder roast, and are suitable for braising or frying.

Sirloin steak, boneless

Boneless sirloin steak is cut from the loin section (in England, the section of loin adjoining the rump) and is suitable for braising, broiling (*grilling*), or frying.

Top loin chops

Top loin chops are loin chops with tenderloin removed. They are from the loin section and are suitable for braising or frying.

Top round steak

This steak is cut from the top of the leg (the round section in the US; the *leg fillet* section in England). It is suitable for braising or frying.

Veal birds

See Scaloppine.

VEAL CUTS, *cont.*

Veal patties	These are veal burgers and are made from ground (*minced*) neck, shoulder, breast, and/or leg meat.
Veal saddle	This section of the animal is comprised of the two loins and part of the rump section (in England, the *loin, rump,* and part of the *leg fillet* section).
Veal stew	Veal stew is made from pieces of boneless meat of varying sizes, usually cut from the shank and shoulder sections (in England, the *foreknuckle,* and *neck* and *shoulder* sections).
Wiener schnitzel	*See Scaloppine.*

Wax paper	use *baking parchment* or *greaseproof paper* Wax paper is not normally available in England, other than for industrial use, although some speciality shops do carry it. You will need to substitute using *baking parchment* or *greaseproof paper.* These are unbleached papers manufactured for kitchen use. The difference between the two is that *baking parchment* is coated with silicone on each side to give it non-stick properties.
Wheat	*Wheat* (or, esp. England, *corn* - see 'Corn' entry)
Wheat berries	*Wheat grains* (also *whole wheat grains*) or *wheat kernels*

Above: *American wax paper.*
Below: *British baking parchment and greaseproof paper.*

Whisk	*Balloon whisk* or *whisk*
Whiskey	*American rye whiskey* In America, 'whiskey' normally refers to rye whiskey (also called simply, 'rye'). In the US, if someone wants scotch whisky, they'll ask for a scotch; for bourbon whiskey, they'll ask for a bourbon (or the brand name, e.g., Jack Daniels). If they don't specify the type, they generally mean 'rye'. Canadian rye whisky is available in England but American rye can be difficult to find other than in speciality shops.
Wholewheat bread	*Wholemeal bread*
Yeast, active dry	*Dried yeast* or *dried active yeast* This is simply compressed yeast which has had most of its moisture removed and, as with compressed yeast, it must first be proofed before being added to your dry ingredients.
Yeast, 'fast-action', 'quick-rise', or 'rapid-rise' dried	Use *'easybake'* or *'easy-blend' dried yeast* Although the most commonly available yeast in England (or in Burton, at any rate) is the 'easy-blend' kind, for some reason the similar 'fast-action' type never caught on in the US. With these yeasts, you don't proof -- simply add them to the dry ingredients, and blend in the warm (or, for 'fast-action' yeast, hot) liquid.
Yogurt, unflavoured	*Natural yogurt*
Zucchini	*Courgettes*

MEASUREMENTS

The Measurements section consists of the following:

Remember that for many of the same words (e.g., pint; gallon), the American and British amounts are not equal, so be sure to look in the correct column. I've listed the British measurements in **boldface** and the metric measurements in *italic.*

In most sections of this book and in the tables that follow, the equivalent amounts listed have been rounded off. (For an exact equivalent, see the Dry Weights and Fluid Volumes Conversion Tables where I've listed the full numbers for calculations.)

By the way, you'll notice that as the UK becomes more and more metric, our product sizes are working their way towards metric-oriented rather than pound-oriented amounts (e.g., 500g rather than 454g [1 lb.]), so keep an eye out for this when shopping.

DRY WEIGHTS (QUICK REFERENCE)

For those of us who are tired of calculating the number of grams in 5 ounces or 28 ounces, etc., I've devised this 'at a glance' chart which should help (it helps me). For weights over 40 ounces, see page 128 for the calculations.

Avoirdupois	Metric	Avoirdupois	Metric
1 oz.	28g	21 oz.	595g
2 oz.	57g	22 oz.	624g
3 oz.	85g	23 oz.	652g
4 oz.	113g	(1½ lb.) 24 oz.	680g
5 oz.	142g	25 oz.	709g
6 oz.	170g	26 oz.	737g
7 oz.	198g	27 oz.	765g
(½ lb.) 8 oz.	227g	28 oz.	794g
9 oz.	255g	29 oz.	822g
10 oz.	283g	30 oz.	850g
11 oz.	312g	31 oz.	879g
12 oz.	340g	(2 lb.) 32 oz.	907g
13 oz.	369g	33 oz.	936g
14 oz.	397g	34 oz.	964g
15 oz.	425g	35 oz.	(~ 1 kg) 992g
(1 lb.) 16 oz.	454g	36 oz.	(1.02 kg) 1020g
17 oz.	482g	37 oz.	(1.05 kg) 1049g
18 oz.	510g	38 oz.	(1.08 kg) 1077g
19 oz.	539g	39 oz.	(1.11 kg) 1106g
20 oz.	567g	(2½ lb.) 40 oz.	(1.13 kg) 1134g

FLUID VOLUME (QUICK REFERENCE)

You'll notice this 'at a glance' chart has separate columns for US and British fluid ounces so be sure to look in the right one (although the slight difference isn't really noticeable until you get up into gallons). For weights over 20 ounces, see page 126 for the calculations.

American	*Metric*	**British**	*Metric*
1 fl. oz.	*30ml*	**1 fl. oz.**	*28ml*
2 fl. oz.	*59ml*	**2 fl. oz.**	*57ml*
3 fl. oz.	*89ml*	**3 fl. oz.**	*85ml*
4 fl. oz.	*118ml*	**4 fl. oz.**	*114ml*
5 fl. oz.	*148ml*	**5 fl. oz.**	*142ml*
6 fl. oz.	*177ml*	**6 fl. oz.**	*170ml*
7 fl. oz.	*207ml*	**7 fl. oz.**	*199ml*
8 fl. oz.	*237ml*	**8 fl. oz.**	*227ml*
9 fl. oz.	*266ml*	**9 fl. oz.**	*256ml*
10 fl. oz.	*296ml*	**10 fl. oz.**	*284ml*
11 fl. oz.	*325ml*	**11 fl. oz.**	*313ml*
12 fl. oz.	*355ml*	**12 fl. oz.**	*341ml*
13 fl. oz.	*384ml*	**13 fl. oz.**	*369ml*
14 fl. oz.	*414ml*	**14 fl. oz.**	*398ml*
15 fl. oz.	*444ml*	**15 fl. oz.**	*426ml*
16 fl. oz.	*473ml*	**16 fl. oz.**	*455ml*
17 fl. oz.	*503ml*	**17 fl. oz.**	*483ml*
18 fl. oz.	*532ml*	**18 fl. oz.**	*511ml*
19 fl. oz.	*562ml*	**19 fl. oz.**	*540ml*
20 fl. oz.	*591ml*	**20 fl. oz.**	*568ml*

MILK CHART

% Fat	British milk	American milk
0.5	⇦ Skimmed Milk: 0.1% avg. fat (max: 0.3%)	Skim or Nonfat Milk: *less than* 0.5% fat
1.0		⇦ 1% Milk Lowfat Milk:
1.5	Semi-skimmed milk (also ⇦ seen as *half-fat milk*): 1.6% avg. fat content	0.5% to 2% fat
2.0	(min: 1.5%; max: 1.8%)	⇦ 2% Milk
2.5		
3.0		
3.5		
4.0	Whole Milk: 3.8-3.9% avg. fat (min: 3.5; max: 4.2%)[15]	Whole Milk: *at least* 3.5% fat (though this amount may vary from state to state in the US)
4.5	Channel Is. Milk (sometimes labelled *Breakfast Milk*):	
5.0	4.8-5.1% avg. fat (min. 4% fat)	

---

[15] *Full cream milk* used to just refer to Channel Islands milk but now has come to mean any whole milk.

CREAM CHART

% Fat	British creams	American creams
10	⇦ Half cream: 12-13% avg. fat ⇦ Half-fat crème fraîche: 15% avg. fat	Half & Half: 10.5 to 11.7% avg. fat (min: 10.5%; max: 18%)
20	⇦ Single cream & Soured cream: 19% avg. fat for single cream (min. 18% fat)	⇦ Sour cream: *at least* 18% — Light or coffee cream: 18% to 30%
30	Crème fraîche: 30-35% fat	Light whipping cream: 30-36% fat Heavy whipping or heavy cream: 36-40%
40	⇦ Whipping cream: 39% avg. fat content (min. 35% fat)	
50	⇦ Double cream: 48% fat	
	Clotted cream: 55%-63.5% avg. fat	

EGG SIZES

British egg sizes are based on a weight per egg. When an American recipe calls for an egg and doesn't specify a size, use an egg weighing about 2 oz. (a Medium egg based on the current EEC egg sizes).

Current EEC Egg Sizes (as of January, 1998)			
Small	Medium	Large	XL or Very Large
under 53 grams	*53-63 grams*	*63-73 grams*	*73g and above*
under 1.87 ounces	1.87-2.22 ounces	2.22-2.57 ounces	2.57 oz. and above

Egg weights courtesy the Ministry of Agriculture, Fisheries, and Food.

Old EEC Egg Sizes (prior to January, 1998)							
7	6	5	4	3	2	1	0
under 45g	*45-50 grams*	*50-55 grams*	*55-60 grams*	*60-65 grams*	*65-70 grams*	*70-75 grams*	*over 75g*
~1.57 oz.	~1.68 oz.	~1.85 oz.	~2 oz.	~2.2 oz.	~2.38 oz.	~2.5 oz.	~2.65 oz.

Egg weights courtesy the British Egg Information Service.

EGG SIZES, continued

American egg sizes are based on a minimum weight per dozen eggs as set by the US Department of Agriculture. The weights below were calculated based on the weight per dozen.

American Egg Sizes				
Small	Medium	Large	Extra large	Jumbo
~43-50g/ egg	*~50-57g/ egg*	*~57-64g/ egg*	*~64-71g/ egg*	*~71g/egg and above*
1.5-2.0 oz./egg	1.75-2.0 oz./egg	2-2.25 oz./egg	2.25-2.5 oz./egg	2.5 oz./egg and above
at least 18 oz./ dozen	at least 21 oz./ dozen	at least 24 oz./ dozen	at least 27 oz./ dozen	at least 30 oz./ dozen

FOOD MASS EQUIVALENTS

I think the thing that causes the greatest aggravation to non-Americans when cooking a recipe intended for the American market, is cups. The weight of a cup of something varies, sometimes significantly (as with courgettes). Even flours vary in weight. In Claudia Roden's *The Book of Jewish Food*, she tells of disparities she encountered when measuring and weighing flour: 500 grams of plain flour equalled anywhere from 3½ to 4 cups. Her advice was to, when necessary, adjust the recipe, adding a little more water or flour, as appropriate. The thing to remember is this: the same ingredients *will* vary in weight; the table below is only a loose guide so, if what you are cooking seems too wet or too dry, adjust the other ingredients until its consistency seems right.

Food	Amount	Equivalent to
Bananas (3-4 medium)	1¾ cups, mashed	1 lb. (*454g*)
Beans, dried (*see Legumes*)		
Beans, fresh green	3-3½ cups	1 lb. (*454g*)
Butter, 1 stick	½ cup (or 8 Tbl.)	4 oz. (*113g*)
Cabbage, shredded	3½-4 cups	1 lb. (*454g*)
Carrots:		
chopped or sliced	3 cups	1 lb. (*454g*)
shredded	2½-3 cups	1 lb. (*454g*)
Celery, chopped or sliced	½ cup	1 medium stalk
Cheese, cottage	1 cup	½ lb. (*227g*)
Cheese, shredded	1 cup	¼ lb. (*113g*)
Cocoa	4 cups	1 lb. (*454g*)
Cornmeal	3 cups	1 lb. (*454g*)
Flour:		
All purpose (*plain*)	4 cups	1 lb. (*454g*)
Wheat (*wholemeal*)	3¾ to 4 cups	1 lb. (*454g*)
Gelatin	1 envelope (or 1 Tbl.)	¼ oz. (*7g*)

FOOD MASS EQUIVALENTS, cont.

Food	Amount	Equivalent to
Graham cracker crumbs	1 cup	15 crackers
Honey	1⅓ cups	1 lb. (*454g*)
Lard	2 cups	1 lb. (*454g*)
Legumes:		
Beans, kidney	2½ cups	1 lb. (*454g*)
Beans, navy	2 cups	1 lb. (*454g*)
Lentils	2¼ cups	1 lb. (*454g*)
Peas, split	2¼ cups	1 lb. (*454g*)
Marshmallows:		
16 large, cut-up	1 cup	4 oz. (*113g*)
90 miniature	1 cup	2 oz. (*56g*)
Mushrooms, sliced	5-6 cups	1 lb. (*454g*)
Nuts	1 cup	5 oz. (*142g*)
Oatmeal (uncooked)	5¾ cups	1 lb. (*454g*)
Onions, chopped	2 to 2½ cups	1 lb. (*454g*) 4 medium onions
Raisins, seedless	2¾ cups	1 lb. (*454g*)
Salt:		
Kosher	¼ cup	1.1 oz. (*30g*)
Regular table salt	¼ cup	2.2 oz. (*60g*)
Sugar:		
Brown, packed	2¼ cups	1 lb. (*454g*)
Confectioners (*Icing*)	3½ to 4 cups	1 lb. (*454g*)
Granulated	2 cups	1 lb. (*454g*)
Wheatgerm	3 cups	12 oz. (*340g*)
Yeast:		
Compressed	1 cake	1 pkg. active dried
Active dried	1 package	1 Tbl. (*appr. 5g*)

AMERICAN COOKING EQUIVALENTS

Keep in mind that when American recipes call for teaspoons and tablespoons, *level* spoonfuls are meant; when British recipes call for teaspoons and tablespoons, *rounded* or *heaping* spoonfuls are meant. Two American (level) tablespoons are roughly equivalent to one British (heaped) tablespoon.

US measure	British measure	US fl. oz.	Metric	Also equal to these US measures
60 drops	1 tsp.			1 tsp.
teaspoon	1 tsp.		*5 ml*	$^1/_3$ Tbl.
	dessert-spoon	$^1/_3$ oz.	*10 ml*	2 tsp. (the US has no dessertspoon measure)
Tablespoon	$^1/_2$ oz.	$^1/_2$ oz.	*15 ml*	3 tsp.
fluid ounce	1 oz.	1 oz.	*30 ml*	2 Tbl.
$^1/_4$ cup	2 oz.	2 oz.	*59 ml*	4 Tbl. *or* $^1/_2$ gill
$^1/_3$ cup	coffee cup	$2^2/_3$ oz.	*79 ml*	$5^1/_3$ Tbl.
$^1/_2$ cup	$^1/_5$ pint	4 oz.	*118 ml*	8 Tbl. *or* 1 gill
1 gill	4 oz.	4 oz.	*118 ml*	$^1/_2$ C *or* 8 Tbl.
$^2/_3$ cup	teacup *or* 1 gill*	$5^1/_3$ oz.	*158 ml*	
$^3/_4$ cup	$6^1/_4$ oz.	6 oz.	*177 ml*	12 Tbl.

---

* In Britain, the gill is 5 oz. (1/4 Brit. pint) but in the north and west of England it is 10 oz. (1/2 Brit. pint).

AMERICAN COOKING EQUIVALENTS, cont.

US measure	British measure	US fl. oz.	*Metric*	Also equal to these US measures
1 cup**	breakfast cup	8 oz.	*237 ml*	½ pt. *or* 2 gills *or* 16 Tbl.
1 pint	~⁴/₅ pint	16 oz.	*473 ml*	2 C *or* ½ qt.
1 quart	33⅓ oz	32 oz.	*946 ml*	4 C *or* 2 pts. *or* ¼ gal.
½ gallon	66⅔ oz	64 oz.	*1.89 l*	4 pts. *or* 2 qts.
1 gallon	133 oz.	128 oz.	*3.78 l*	8 pts. *or* 4 qts.

Note: tsp.=teaspoon; Tbl. or T.=tablespoon; C=cup; pt.=pint; qt.=quart; and gal.=gallon. Also, *ml=millilitre* and *l=litre*.

AMERICAN CAN SIZES

Can size	Equivalent Weights
No. 300	14-16 ounces *(395-455g)*
No. 303	16-17 ounces *(455-480g)*
No. 2	1 lb., 4 oz. (i.e., 20 oz.) *(565g)* *or* 1 US pint, 2 fl. oz. (i.e., 18 oz.) *(530ml)*
No. 2½	1 lb., 13 oz. (i.e., 29 oz.) *(820g)*
No. 3	46 ounces *(1.3kg)*

** The British standard cup is 10 ounces but ordinary cups are more commonly used in British kitchens.

FLUID VOLUMES & CONVERSION TABLES

A fluid ounce is a measure of *volume* rather than weight so the weight of a fluid ounce will vary according to the density of the substance being weighed. The volume, however, will not vary and litres, centilitres, and millilitres are measures of volume.

1 US ounce = *29.57 millilitres*
1 US pint = 16 US ounces
1 US quart = 2 US pints = 32 US ounces
1 US gallon = 4 quarts = 8 US pints = 128 US ounces

1 British ounce = *28.41 millilitres*
1 British pint = 20 British ounces
1 British gallon = 8 British pints = 160 British ounces

1 litre = 100 centilitres = 1,000 millilitres

The following tables convert American, British, and metric fluid volumes.

TO CONVERT FROM METRIC:

From:	To:	Multiply by:
millilitres	US fl. ounce	0.03381497
millilitres	US pint	0.002113436
millilitres	**British fl. ounce**	0.03519609
millilitres	**British pint**	0.001759804
centilitres	US fl. ounce	0.3381497
centilitres	US pint	0.02113436
centilitres	**British fl. ounce**	0.3519609
centilitres	**British pint**	0.01759804
litres	US fl. ounce	33.81497
litres	US gallon	0.2641794
litres	**British fl. ounce**	35.19609
litres	**Imperial gallon**	0.2199755

Fluid Volume Conversion Tables, cont.

To Convert from American:

From:	To:	Multiply by:
fl. ounce (US)	**British fl. ounce**	1.040843
fl. ounce (US)	*millilitres*	29.57
fl. ounce (US)	*litres*	0.029572702
pint (US)	**British pint**	1.2009638
pint (US)	*millilitres*	473.12
pint (US)	*litres*	.47312
gallon (US)	**Imperial gallon**	0.83267
gallon (US)	*litres*	3.785306

To Convert from British (Imperial):

From:	To:	Multiply by:
fl. ounce (British)	US fl. ounce	0.9607594
fl. ounce (British)	*millilitres*	28.41
fl. ounce (British)	*litres*	0.02841225
pint (British)	US pint	.8326645
pint (British)	*millilitres*	568.2
pint (British)	*litres*	.5682
gallon (Imperial)	US gallon	1.20095
gallon (Imperial)	*litres*	4.546

DRY WEIGHTS & DRY WEIGHT CONVERSION TABLES

With the exception of large commercial weights and the fact that the American system has no stone,* dry weights are the same for the US and the UK, so 1 US lb. (avoirdupois) = 1 British lb. (avoirdupois).

1 ounce = *28.35 grams = 2835 milligrams*

1 pound = 16 ounces = *454 grams = .454 kilograms*

1 kilogram = 1,000 grams = 1,000,000 milligrams

TO CONVERT *TO* METRIC:

From:	To:	Multiply by:
ounces (avoirdupois)	*grams*	28.349523
ounces (avoirdupois)	*kilograms*	0.0283
pounds (avoirdupois)	*grams*	453.59237
pounds (avoirdupois)	*kilograms*	0.45359237

TO CONVERT *FROM* METRIC:

From:	To:	Multiply by:
grams	ounces (avoirdupois)	0.035273962
kilograms	pounds (avoirdupois)	2.2046

---

* A stone equals 14 pounds.

LINEAR MEASURE*

1 inch = *2.54 centimetres*
1 foot = *30. 48 centimetres*
1 yard = *91.44 centimetres or .9 metre*

1 centimetre = 0.39 inch
1 metre = 39.37 inches

1 millimetre = .1 centimetre
1 centimetre = 10 millimetres
1 metre = 100 centimetres or 1,000 millimetres or 0.001 kilometres
1 kilometre = 1,000 metres

TO CONVERT *TO* METRIC:

From:	To:	Multiply by:
inches	*centimetres*	2.54
feet	*centimetres*	30.4801
yards	*metres*	0.914
miles	*kilometres*	1.609

TO CONVERT *FROM* METRIC:

From:	To:	Multiply by:
centimetres	inches	0.39370079
centimetres	feet	0.0328
metres	yards	1.094

---

* There is no difference between British and American inches, feet and yards.

TEMPERATURES

OVEN TEMPERATURES

Fahrenheit	*Celsius**	Gas Mark	Descriptions
225	*110*	¼	
250	*120*	½	very slow
275	*135*	1	
300	*150*	2	slow
325	*160*	3	moderately slow
350	*175*	4	moderate
375	*190*	5	moderately hot
400	*205*	6	hot
425	*220*	7	
450	*230*	8	very hot
475	*245*	9	
500	*260*	10	extremely hot**

---

* The Celsius temperatures listed in this chart are approximate equivalents to their corresponding Fahrenheit temperatures.

** This is the temperature bakers use to bake bread rolls; it is too hot for home baking.

TEMPERATURES, continued

AIR TEMPERATURES

Fahrenheit	Celsius		Fahrenheit	Celsius
32	*0*		149	*65*
41	*5*		158	*70*
50	*10*		167	*75*
59	*15*		176	*80*
68	*20*		185	*85*
77	*25*		194	*90*
86	*30*		203	*95*
95	*35*		212	*100*
104	*40*		221	*105*
113	*45*		230	*110*
122	*50*		239	*115*
131	*55*		248	*120*
140	*60*		257	*125*

To convert Fahrenheit to *Celsius*, subtract 32; and then divide by 1.8.

To convert *Celsius* to Fahrenheit, multiply by 1.8; and then add 32.

RECIPES

Some of the recipes included in this section originated from countries other than the United States but I've included them because they've become part of the standard American cuisine.

I've listed the ingredients in an order I hope is not confusing. When recipe books list the American, British, and metric measurements all together, it's easy to read the wrong one. So to avoid this, I've listed first the American ingredients set off in a box; followed by the British ingredients, together with both the British and metric measures. (In cases where there is little difference, only the British and metric measurements are listed.)

You may notice that sometimes the American amounts do not exactly equal the British amounts. This is usually because the original recipe is based on the size of a bottle or box; etc. that's sold in the US and which doesn't exactly correspond to the sizes available in England. In such cases, I've adapted the recipes to the sizes available in England.

For very small amounts (e.g., 1 teaspoon) where the low weight would be difficult to measure, an equivalent British and metric weight are not given. Instead, I recommend purchasing a set of measuring spoons, in ¼ teaspoon, ½ teaspoon, 1 teaspoon (*5 ml*), and 1 tablespoon (*15 ml*) sizes. Note that unless otherwise stated, all measurements (e.g. teaspoon, cup, etc.) are *level* measurements -- not heaped.

Keep in mind that the liquid amounts for the UK and US differ in ounces, pints, and gallons so always consult the Measurements Section whenever there is a question.

All of these recipes have been 'home-tested' in England.

RECIPE LIST

SALADS AND DRESSINGS

GREEN SALAD

In England, the word salad often refers to a combination of cress, cucumber, and tomato, sans any dressing, and served more as a garnish than a side dish. In the US, it's not uncommon for a salad to be the main dish (often with the mistaken belief that, even drowned in dressing, it's a low-calorie meal). When you find yourself sliding into a lettuce/cucumber/tomato salad rut, check the list below to see what a salad could be, if you'd only let it.

Ingredients	
	• greens (e.g., lettuce; spinach)
	• onion, thinly sliced (around a quarter of an onion)
	• cheese, shredded (around a quarter pound [*115 g*])
	• raw vegetables, grated or chopped (e.g. a mixture of the following)

        carrots   *red or green peppers*
        courgettes   *cauliflower*
        beetroot   *broccoli*
        green beans   *cucumbers*
        radishes   *celery*

• for the garnish, a mixture of sliced or chopped raw vegetables, nuts, etc., e.g.:

        tomatoes   *olives (green or black)*
        mushrooms   *hard boiled eggs, sliced*
        avocado   *sunflower seeds &/or raisins*
        chives or scallions (green onions)

For the dressing, use any dressing you like.

Procedure	
	Wash the greens and remove any discoloured or wilted leaves. Shred them into bite-sized pieces and spin dry in a salad spinner (or dry with a towel).
	Prepare the vegetables, onion, cheese and garnish.

In a large bowl, combine everything but the garnish and toss. Add salad dressing to taste and thoroughly combine.

Decorate the salad with garnish(es) of your choice and serve.

COLESLAW   serves 12

Ingredients with the original American measurements:

1 small head green cabbage

1 tablespoon kosher salt

3 medium carrots (or 2 large)

1 stalk celery

chopped fresh parsley or chives, optional

Dressing: ½ cup sour cream

2 tablespoons cider vinegar

½ teaspoon grated onion

2 teaspoons kosher salt

½ teaspoon coarsely ground pepper

1 tablespoon sugar

Ingredients with British measurements (*followed by metric*):

1 small head white cabbage

1 tablespoon kosher salt (or 1½ teaspoons table salt)

3 medium carrots (or 2 large)

1 stalk celery

chopped fresh parsley or chives, optional

Dressing:

    5 oz. soured cream or single cream   (*140 ml*)

    2 tablespoons cider vinegar

    ½ teaspoon grated onion

    2 teaspoons kosher salt (or 1 teaspoon table salt)

    ½ teaspoon coarsely ground pepper

    1 tablespoon sugar

Procedure

Note: Although the preparation doesn't take long, the cabbage needs an hour to macerate, so don't forget to allow for that when planning your time.

Remove any wilted outer leaves of the cabbage. Cut the cabbage into quarters and core it. Finely cut the cabbage into thin shreds, toss them into a colander, and rinse under cold water.

Place the cabbage in a large bowl and sprinkle it with the salt. Fill the bowl with enough cold water to cover the cabbage. Leave it to macerate for 1 hour.

While the cabbage is macerating, peel and shred the carrots on a grater (or better yet, a food processor). Mince the celery. Chop the parsley and/or chives, if you are using them. Set all this aside.

Combine the dressing ingredients and set that aside.

After an hour, drain the cabbage. Add the vegetables and toss. Give the dressing a good shake and add that. Combine thoroughly and serve.

MACARONI SALAD *serves 10-12*

There are any number of recipes for macaroni salad but this is one of my favourites -- if I make it once, I make it three times. Something in its combination of flavours brings out the taste of summer so it's a good one to make on those cold, rainy, overcast days in June to remind yourself that, according to the calendar at least, summer has begun.

Ingredients with the original American measurements:

2 cups uncooked macaroni

6 tablespoons vinaigrette or oil & vinegar mixture

½ cup minced fresh parsley

1 teaspoon dried basil (or 1 tablespoon fresh)

½ cup toasted pinenuts

2 cups chopped celery with leaves

3 to 4 tablespoons chopped chives

½ cup chopped pimiento

lettuce

watercress for garnish, optional

Ingredients with British measurements *(followed by metric)*:

9 oz. uncooked macaroni *(255 g)*

6 tablespoons vinaigrette (recipe follows)
    or oil & vinegar mixture

6 heaped tablespoons minced fresh parsley

1 teaspoon dried basil (or 1 tablespoon fresh)

3 oz. toasted pinenuts *(85 g)* (recipe follows)

8 oz. chopped celery with leaves *(225 g)*

3 to 4 tablespoons chopped chives

6 heaped tablespoons chopped pimiento*
(or, if you can't find pimiento, a red sweet pepper
prepared according to the instructions that follow)

lettuce

watercress for garnish, optional

Procedure   Cook the macaroni according to package instructions.
In a large bowl, combine the drained macaroni and the
vinaigrette. Cover and put in the fridge to chill for one
hour.
Once chilled, add the remaining ingredients and mix
thoroughly. Add salt and pepper to taste.
Serve on a bed of lettuce and garnish with watercress.

The recipe for vinaigrette:

Combine: ¼ cup white wine vinegar (2 oz. or *60 ml*)
½ cup olive oil (4 oz. or *120 ml*)
1 teaspoon Dijon mustard
1 tablespoon lemon juice
1 clove garlic, crushed
salt & pepper to taste

Instructions for toasting pinenuts:

Heat on high a dry frying pan (don't add oil -- you're toasting the
pinenuts *dry*).

Add the pinenuts and shake frequently until the nuts are lightly
browned. Immediately remove the nuts from the pan to prevent them
burning.

* Pimiento is a variety of red sweet pepper and is easily obtained in the US
(sold usually in small jars). I've never seen it in England although I've read
that it is sold here, usually in cans and often labelled *pimento*.

Instructions for preparing the red sweet pepper:

To loosen its skin, you may either boil or broil (*grill*) it. To boil, drop the pepper into boiling water and simmer 20-25 minutes. (Otherwise broil [*grill*] it 1½ - 2" [*4-5cm*] from the heat for around 25 minutes, turning it as the skin blackens.) When cool enough to handle, peel the skin and remove the stalk, seeds, and membranes. Chop the pepper and set aside what you need. Refrigerate any that's left over.

POTATO SALAD

Although potato salad is considered a summer dish, I see no reason why this shouldn't be allowed to add colour and taste to what's too often a stodgy winter meal. When the days are short or when it's so overcast it looks like dusk at noon, try this and bring your taste buds out of hibernation.

Ingredients with the original American measurements:

4 to 5 cups cooked sliced new potatoes

4 hard cooked eggs, sliced

2 cups cooked green beans (optional)

3 stalks celery, finely chopped

2 tablespoons grated onion

Dressing: set aside: ¾ cup olive oil;
              combine: ¼ cup vinegar
                         1 large clove garlic, crushed
                         1 tablespoon lemon juice
                         1 teaspoon horseradish
                         1 teaspoon Dijon mustard

¾ cup sliced pimiento

1 teas. salt and ½ teas. pepper (more or less to taste)

leaf lettuce

Ingredients with British measurements (*followed by metric*):

6 medium new potatoes (around 1½ lbs. or *680 g*)

4 hard cooked eggs, sliced

6 to 7 oz. cooked green beans, optional (*170-200g*)

3 stalks celery, finely chopped

2 tablespoons grated onion

Dressing: Set aside: 6 oz. olive oil (*180 ml*)
                   Combine: 2 oz. vinegar (*120 ml*)
                                1 large clove garlic, crushed
                                1 tablespoon lemon juice
                                1 teaspoon horseradish
                                1 teaspoon Dijon mustard

4½ oz. sliced pimiento (*125 g*)
    (or, if you can't find pimiento, a red sweet pepper
    prepared according to the instructions that follow)

1 teaspoon salt (more or less to taste)

½ teaspoon pepper (more or less to taste)

leaf lettuce

Procedure   Note: This potato salad needs one hour to marinate, so
don't forget to allow for that when planning your time.

First, start these cooking:
- Cook whole potatoes in their skins. Simmer 20-25
  minutes or until tender.
- Hard boil the eggs: put eggs in water and bring to
  a boil; then turn off heat, cover, and leave for 15
  minutes; then remove the eggs and set aside.
- If using a red pepper, prepare it now by either
  boiling or broiling (*grilling*) it. To boil, drop the
  pepper into boiling water and simmer 20-25
  minutes. (Otherwise broil [*grill*] it 1½ - 2"

[*4-5cm*] from the heat for around 25 minutes, turning it as the skin blackens.)

While the above is cooking, prepare these:

- If including green beans, cut the green beans into 1" pieces (*2.5cm*) and steam for 10 minutes
- Chop the celery and grate the onion.
- Prepare the dressing: Slowly pour the olive oil into the vinegar mixture and whisk it to combine.

When the above has finished cooking:

- Shell and slice the hard boiled eggs.
- Peel and slice the cooked potatoes.
- And if using a red pepper, peel the pepper (once it's cool enough to handle), and remove its stalk, seeds, and membrane. Slice thinly and chop.

In a large bowl, combine the warm potatoes; celery; onion; eggs; beans (if including them); pimiento (or red pepper); salt and pepper.

Gently heat the dressing and pour that over the combined ingredients.

Cover and let marinate one hour.

Give a final mix and serve on leaf lettuce.

FRENCH SALAD DRESSING (AMERICAN STYLE)

In the US, when someone says "French dressing", they usually mean a bright orange (almost luminescent), slightly sweet, bottled dressing. If you like sweet and sour dishes, then this is the dressing for you.

> Ingredients with the original American measurements:
>
> ¾ cup vegetable oil
> ¼ cup lemon juice or vinegar
> ¼ cup ketchup
> 8 drops Worcestershire sauce
> 1 teaspoon sugar
> 1 teaspoon honey (or another of sugar)
> salt and pepper
> optional: paprika and herbs (e.g., tarragon) to taste

Ingredients with British measurements (*followed by metric*):

6 oz. vegetable oil   (*180 ml*)

2 oz. lemon juice or vinegar   (*60 ml*)

2 oz. ketchup   (*60 ml*)

8 drops Worcestershire sauce

1 teaspoon sugar

1 teaspoon honey (or another of sugar)

salt and pepper to taste

optional: paprika and herbs (e.g., tarragon) to taste

Procedure   Whisk the oil and vinegar.

Add the remaining ingredients and shake well.

Pour on green salad and serve.

RUSSIAN DRESSING   *makes about 1 cup (8 oz. or 220 gr)*

Russian dressing and Thousand Island dressing are very similar. So far, I've only seen Thousand Island dressing in England. A Reuben sandwich is made with Russian dressing so, if you're making a Reuben sandwich and want to be a purist, here's a recipe for Russian dressing.

Ingredients with the original American measurements:

¾ cup mayonnaise

¼ cup chili sauce or ketchup

1 tablespoon grated horseradish

1 tablespoon finely chopped green pepper

1 teaspoon Worcestershire sauce

1 teaspoon grated onion or finely chopped chives

Ingredients with British measurements (*followed by metric*):

6 oz. mayonnaise   (*165 g*)

2 oz. chili sauce or ketchup   (*55 g*)

1 tablespoon grated horseradish

1 tablespoon finely chopped green pepper

1 teaspoon Worcestershire sauce

1 teaspoon grated onion or finely chopped chives

Procedure   Combine above ingredients and chill. Use as salad dressing or in place of mayonnaise in sandwiches.

SANDWICHES

CHICKEN SALAD SANDWICHES *makes 7 to 8 servings*

English and American chicken salad sandwiches are different: English ones are made with chicken meat and salad greens (and maybe tomato) while American ones use a mayonnaise-based mixture of chopped chicken, celery and walnuts. You can make the following recipe with walnuts but I highly recommend trying it with the toasted sesame seeds -- that never fails to draw compliments and requests for the recipe.

Ingredients with the original American measurements:

4 cups cooked chopped chicken

2 medium stalks celery, finely chopped

2 tablespoons sesame seeds, toasted
(or ½ cup chopped walnuts, toasted)

2 tablespoons parsley, minced

2 tablespoons watercress, minced

mayonnaise

salt and pepper to taste

lettuce

Ingredients with British measurements (*followed by metric*):

20 oz. cooked chopped chicken (*565 g*)

2 medium stalks celery, finely chopped

2 tablespoons sesame seeds, toasted
(or 3 oz. chopped walnuts, toasted [*85 g*])

2 tablespoons parsley, minced

2 tablespoons watercress, minced

mayonnaise

salt and pepper to taste

lettuce

Procedure   If starting with raw chicken, put it in a frying pan and add water and/or white wine to partially cover the chicken. Cover the pan and simmer the chicken until tender. Allow the chicken to cool before chopping or shredding it.

To toast the seeds or nuts, heat a dry frying pan on high. Once hot, add the sesame seeds or walnuts and shake the pan frequently to keep them from burning. Continue to shake the pan over the flame for a few minutes or until the seeds have started to smoke and give off a toasted aroma. Immediately pour them into a dish and set aside; don't leave them in the hot pan or they will burn.

In a large bowl, combine the chicken, celery, sesame seeds (or walnuts), parsley, and watercress and toss.

Stir in enough mayonnaise to make the mixture hold together.

Add salt and pepper to taste. Serve with lettuce in a sandwich or French stick, or alone on a bed of lettuce.

SALMON SALAD SANDWICHES

Ingredients   *418 g* tin of red salmon

2 stalks celery, minced

herbs: 1 tablespoon fresh minced parsley
¼ teaspoon dried tarragon (or ½ tsp. fresh)
1 tablespoon fresh minced chives
1 tablespoon fresh minced watercress

mayonnaise

½ tablespoon *double concentrated tomato puree* (tomato paste)

1 tablespoon lemon juice (preferably from fresh lemon)

Procedure   Remove undesirable bits from the tinned salmon.

Mince the celery and herbs.

In a large bowl, combine everything except the mayonnaise.

When the mixture is fully combined, add enough mayonnaise to make a paste, and mix thoroughly.

Serve with lettuce in sandwiches.

REUBEN SANDWICHES

It's expensive to make these sandwiches in England (check out how much *salt beef* you get for £1), but when you do decide to splash out, they're a real treat, especially for homesick Americans.

American ingredients:
sliced rye or sour dough rye bread (not sweet rye)
butter
thinly sliced corned beef
sauerkraut
thinly sliced Swiss cheese
Russian dressing

British ingredients:

sliced rye or sour dough rye bread
(See recipe, page 153.)

butter

thinly sliced cooked brisket or salt beef

sauerkraut

thinly sliced Gruyère cheese

Russian dressing   (see recipe in this section)

Procedure   Lightly butter the outsides of the bread.

Layer the beef, sauerkraut, and cheese on one half of
the sandwich. Spread this generously with Russian
dressing and close the sandwich with the remaining
bread (buttered side facing out).

To brown the sandwiches on the stovetop (*hob*), heat a
frying pan to medium-hot and lay in the sandwiches.
Lightly brown one side and carefully turn the
sandwiches over to brown the other side. Once the
cheese has melted, remove from heat.

BREADS, BISCUITS, ETC.

PUMPERNICKEL BREAD   *makes 2 large loaves*

Making bread is an involved, time-consuming process so, in an effort to create a pumpernickel bread I felt was worth the bother, I tried numerous combinations. One day, after baking rye bread made with beer, and this pumpernickel bread made with potato water, I asked my husband to guess which one contained the beer. He chose the pumpernickel, and I'd have said the same if I didn't already know. Intrigued? See what you think.

Ingredients with the original American measurements:
2 teaspoons sugar
5 ounces warm water (110°F)
4 packages (4 tablespoons) active dried yeast
4 cups all purpose flour
4 cups rye flour
1 tablespoon kosher salt
½ cup cornmeal
2 tablespoons molasses
2 tablespoons cocoa powder
2 tablespoons melted butter or oil
2¼ cups water from the potatoes (lukewarm)
2 med. to large potatoes, mashed (room temperature)
1-2 teaspoons freshly-grated orange peel
a little melted butter for glazing

Ingredients with British measurements (*followed by metric*):

>   2 teaspoons sugar
>
>   ¼ pint (5 ounces or *150ml*) warm water (43°C)
>
>   20g active dried baking yeast
>
>   1 pound plain flour   (*454g*)
>
>   1 pound rye flour   (*454g*)
>
>   1 tablespoon kosher salt (or 1½ teaspoons table salt)
>
>   2²/₃ ounces coarse polenta (*76g*)
>
>   1 tablespoon treacle
>
>   1 tablespoon glucose syrup
>
>   2 tablespoons cocoa powder
>
>   2 tablespoons (1 ounce) melted butter or oil (*30g*)
>
>   18 ounces water from the potatoes (lukewarm)
>   (*530ml*)
>
>   2 med. to large potatoes, mashed (room temperature)
>
>   1-2 teaspoons freshly-grated orange peel
>
>   a little melted butter for glazing

Procedure   In a small warm bowl, dissolve the sugar in the warm water. Sprinkle the yeast onto this and whisk it in. Cover the bowl with plastic wrap (*cling film*) and leave it in a warm, draught-free place until the mixture is frothy (10-15 minutes).

In the mean time, peel, cut-up, and boil the potatoes. Drain the potato water into a measuring jug up to the 18 ounce mark (*530ml*); top it up with extra water if it falls short. Add the molasses (or *treacle* and *glucose syrup*), cocoa, and melted butter (or oil) to the potato water.

Mash the potatoes and set them aside.

In a large bowl, combine the plain and rye flour.

In a very large bowl, combine the salt, cornmeal (*polenta*), and 2 cups of the flour mixture. To this, add and stir in the yeast mixture, and then gradually add and stir in the potato water mixture. Next, add the mashed potatoes and enough flour to make a thick batter, and thoroughly combine. Then add the freshly-grated orange peel and enough flour to make a soft dough -- you'll reach a point where you'll have to knead, rather than stir in the flour. Add the remaining flour, ½ cup at a time, until the dough is pliable and not too sticky (add more plain flour if necessary). At this point, you should knead the dough for 15 minutes (however, if it took you longer than 15 minutes [as it always does me] to knead in all the remaining flour, then don't bother to knead it further -- just proceed to the next step).

Find a bowl large enough to fit double the size of the dough. Warm the bowl (e.g., under hot water). Lightly grease the inside of the bowl. Form the dough into a ball and place it in the bowl, turning the dough to coat all sides of it. Cover the bowl with plastic wrap (*cling film*) or a cloth and set in a warm, draught-free spot until it has doubled in size (1 to 2 hours).

While the dough is rising, lightly butter two baking sheets.

When the dough has doubled in size, punch it down (*knock it back*) and then knead it briefly (around 1 minute). Divide the dough in half, shape each half into a round loaf, and place them on the greased baking sheets. Cover each with a cloth, return them to the warm, draught-free spot and let rise until doubled in bulk (30-45 minutes).

Halfway through the second rising, turn the oven on to 190°C or Gas mark 5 (375°F).

When the loaves have doubled from their second rising, place them in the preheated oven. (Note: If your oven is small, then put just one loaf in to bake and leave the other loaf in the warm, draft-free spot. Once the first loaf is done, remove it from the oven and put the second loaf in to bake.) After the loaves have baked for 30 minutes, remove them from the oven, coat them with butter, and then return them to the oven to bake a further 5 minutes. Tap the bottom of the loaves -- if they sound hollow, they're done. Remove them from the oven, coat them again with butter, and leave them to cool on wire racks. Once cool, slice and butter the bread or use it in sandwiches.

RYE BREAD   *makes 2 loaves*

When I began this book, rye bread wasn't sold in English supermarkets.
Now, although it is often available, the rye bread I've found here is not
the dense rye I'm used to, so for a rye bread you can slice almost paper-
thin, try this.

Ingredients with the original American measurements:

For yeast mixture:
    1 teaspoon sugar
    ½ cup warm water (110°-115°F)
    1½ packages (1½ tablespoons) active dried yeast
3 cups rye flour
3½ - 4½ cups plain flour
1 cup boiling water (or potato water)
1 cup milk
2 tablespoons butter or oil
1½ tablespoons dark brown sugar (or 1 tablespoon
    light brown sugar & 1 tablespoon treacle)
1 tablespoon kosher salt (or ½ tablespoon table salt)
1½ tablespoons caraway seeds
For glaze:
    1 egg white, lightly beaten with 1 tablespoon water

Ingredients with British measurements (*followed by metric*):

> For yeast mixture:
> 1 teaspoon sugar
> 4 ounces (*120ml*) warm water (43°-46°C)
> 1½ tablespoons dried active baking yeast
>   (¾ ounce or *20g*)

¾ lb. rye flour   (*340g*)

14 to 18 oz. plain flour   (*397 to 510g*)

8 ounces boiling water (or potato water)   (*237ml*)

8 ounces milk   (*237ml*)

2 tablespoons butter or oil (1 ounce or *30 g*)

1½ tablespoons dark brown sugar (or 1 tablespoon
     light brown sugar & 1 tablespoon treacle)

1 tablespoon kosher salt (or ½ tablespoon table salt)

1½ tablespoons caraway seeds

For glaze:
> 1 egg white, lightly beaten with 1 tablespoon water

Procedure   In a small warm bowl, dissolve the sugar in the warm
water. Sprinkle the yeast onto this and whisk it in.
Cover the bowl with plastic wrap (*cling film*) and leave
it in a warm, draught-free place until the mixture is
frothy (10-15 minutes).

Into a large warm bowl, pour the cup of boiling water
(or potato water). Add the butter (or oil), the brown
sugar, and salt, and stir to combine. (If the butter isn't
melting fast enough, pinch it into smaller pieces.) Add
the cup of milk and the caraway seeds and stir. Add
the rye flour and the yeast mixture and stir to
thoroughly combine. Start adding the plain flour, a
half cup at a time, eventually kneading it in when
stirring is no longer possible. Continue kneading the

dough until it is smooth and no longer sticky (5-10 minutes).

Find a bowl large enough to fit double the size of the dough and grease the inside of that bowl. Form the dough into a ball and place it in the bowl, turning the dough to coat all sides of it. Cover the bowl with a cloth and set it in a warm, draught-free spot. Let it rise until 'doubled in bulk' (1 to 2 hours). To test whether it's doubled in bulk, press 2 fingers into the dough, about ½" deep; if the impressions remain in the dough, then it's risen enough.

While the dough is rising, lightly butter two baking sheets or loaf tins.

Once the dough has doubled in size, punch it down (*knock it back*) and then knead it briefly (around 1 minute). Divide the dough in half, shape each half into a loaf, and place on the greased baking sheets or in the loaf tins. Cover them and return them to the warm, draught-free spot to rise until doubled in bulk again (30-45 minutes).

Halfway through the second rising, turn the oven on to 190°C or Gas mark 5 (375°F).

When the loaves have doubled from their second rising, brush them with the egg mixture and place in the preheated oven. Bake until lightly browned and they sound hollow when tapped on the bottom (around 30 minutes).

Let them cool on a wire rack before slicing.

Serve with butter or use to make sandwiches. (See Recipes Section, *Rueben Sandwich*.)

BAGELS   *makes 18 bagels*

You can usually find frozen bagels in English supermarkets and, occasionally, fresh as well, but for the bagels that remind you of home, you'll have to roll up your sleeves. They're a bit of work, but in the end you've got the real thing (chewy, not spongy).

Ingredients:	6 cups (approx. 1½ lb.) of already-sifted strong bread flour (*~680 g*)
	1 tablespoon kosher salt (or 2 teaspoons table salt)
	1 envelope easy-blend dried yeast
	2 tablespoons sugar (white or brown)
	roughly 1½ cups (12 oz.) warm water (*355 ml*)
Have ready:	2 large bowls (one lightly oiled)
	a floured surface for kneading, and a rolling pin
	cling film (plastic wrap)
	a timer
	a warm, draught-free place for the dough to rise
	baking sheets, lightly dusted with polenta (cornmeal) (or else lightly-oiled)
	a knife to cut the dough into 18 pieces
	a large pot of water -- around 1 gallon (*4 litres*)
	a tablespoon of sugar to add to the pot of water
	a slotted spoon for lifting the bagels
	racks for draining the bagels
Procedure	Sift and measure the flour into a large bowl. Stir in the salt, yeast, and sugar.
	Gradually work in just enough warm water to get the dough to hold together in a ball (adjust flour or water, if necessary). Place the ball on a lightly-floured

surface and knead until it is smooth and elastic (around 10 minutes).

Put the dough into the lightly-oiled bowl and turn the dough around until it's greased all over. Cover the bowl with cling film and place in a warm, draught-free place to rise, until it has 'doubled in bulk' (30-45 minutes). To see if it's risen enough, press two fingers lightly into the dough; if the imprint remains, then the dough is ready.

Punch the dough down (*knock it back*) and knead again briefly. Roll the dough out to a roughly rectangular shape and cut the dough into 18 equal parts. Shape each piece into a rope and overlap the ends, pressing them firmly together to form a ring.

Place the bagels onto the lightly-dusted (or lightly-oiled) baking sheets and let them rise (*prove*) for 20-30 minutes (don't cover them).

Preheat the oven to 190°C or Gas mark 5 (375°F). At the same time, add the sugar to the pot of water and start that boiling.

When the bagels are ready, lower the flame under the water until it is *almost* boiling. Drop the bagels in 1 at a time (do up to 4 together). Cook for 2 minutes on one side and, using your slotted spoon, turn them over and cook an additional 2 minutes on the other side. Lift the bagels out of the water and let them drain on a rack for a minute or so.

Next, place the drained bagels on the lightly-dusted (or lightly-oiled) baking sheets. For the typical fan-assisted ovens, place the baking sheet on the centre rack and, halfway through the baking, turn the sheet around (to ensure even browning on top). Bake 20-30 minutes or until golden on top.

Above: Shaping the bagels. Below: Bagels boiling prior to baking.

| MEXICAN CORNBREAD | *makes two 9" x 9" pans (23 x 23cm)* |

In the 1970s, a co-worker of mine brought in a batch of cornbread which she'd made from a James Beard recipe. I asked for a copy of the recipe and have been making it ever since (and in turn, am always asked for the recipe). My compliments to, and apologies to, James Beard but I've not had a better cornbread than this so why change it? By the way, I've never found fresh Jalapeño chiles in England so, if you can find them bottled, use that. Otherwise, use a different type of *very* hot chiles.

Ingredients with the original American measurements:

2½ cups cornmeal
1 cup all-purpose flour
2 tablespoons sugar
1 tablespoon salt
4 teaspoons baking powder
½ cup non-fat dry milk
3 eggs, room temperature
1½ cups warm water (110°)
½ cup oil
one 1-lb. can creamed corn
6-8 Jalapeño chiles, chopped
2 cups sharp Cheddar cheese, shredded
1 large onion, grated

Ingredients with British measurements (*followed by metric*):

>   11½ oz. coarse polenta (*330 g*)
>
>   5 oz. plain flour (*140 g*)
>
>   1 oz. sugar (*30 g*)
>
>   1 level tablespoon salt (*15 g*)
>
>   4 level teaspoons baking powder
>
>   1½ oz. dried skimmed milk (*40 g*)
>
>   3 eggs, room temperature
>
>   12 oz. warm water (43°C) (*355 ml*)
>
>   4 oz. oil (*120 ml*)
>
>   one *425 g* can cream-style sweetcorn (or a can of
>   regular sweetcorn which you can cream yourself --
>   see directions at end of recipe)
>
>   6-8 Jalapeño (or other hot) chiles, chopped
>
>   ½ lb. mature Cheddar cheese, shredded (*230 g*)
>
>   1 large onion, grated

Procedure   Preheat oven to 220°C or Gas mark 7 (425°F).

Grease two 9" x 9" (*23 cm x 23 cm*) or 9" x 11" (*23 cm x 28 cm*) pans. Alternatively, ungreased teflon pans may be used.

Carefully chop the chiles, preferably wearing rubber gloves. Avoid touching your eyes if any juice from the chiles has gotten on your fingers.

If you are creaming the corn yourself, do that now, following the directions below.

Shred the cheese and grate the onion.

In a large bowl, combine the cornmeal, flour, sugar, salt, baking powder and milk.

In a smaller bowl, lightly beat the eggs, and stir in the water and oil. Pour this mixture into the cornmeal mixture, and stir in the corn, chopped chiles, cheese and grated onion.

Pour the batter into the pans and spread evenly.

Bake in the preheated oven until a wooden toothpick inserted in the centre comes out clean -- usually around 30 minutes.

To cream corn: To substitute for a *425g* can of creamed corn, do the following: Drain the liquid from a can of regular sweetcorn into a measuring cup. Top up that liquid with water until you have 9 ounces (*255g*). Dissolve 1 tablespoon *cornflour* (cornstarch) in 2 tablespoons of water and set aside. In a saucepan, heat the corn and the 9 ounces of liquid. Add the *cornflour* mixture and stir until thickened. Remove from heat and let it cool before including in this recipe.

BISCUITS   *makes about 16-20 biscuits*

These are the type of biscuits served with chicken and gravy, and go well with any gravy or sauce-based dish -- just break them in half and pour the gravy or creamed peas and onions, or whatever, over them. They're fairly similar to a plain English scone (one that's not sweet).

Ingredients with the original American measurements:
2 cups sifted all purpose flour
4 teaspoons baking powder
½ teaspoon salt
½ cup shortening
⅔ cup milk

Ingredients with British measurements (*followed by metric*):

> ¹/₂ lb. sifted plain flour (*280 g*)
>
> 4 teaspoons baking powder
>
> ¹/₂ teaspoon salt
>
> 4 oz. white vegetable fat (e.g., white Flora) (*120 ml*)
>
> 5²/₃ oz. milk (*160 ml*)

Procedure

Preheat the oven to 230°C or Gas mark 8 (450°F).

Sift and *then* measure the flour. Add the baking powder and salt, and combine.

Cut the shortening into the flour mixture until it is crumbly. Make a well in the centre, add the milk and mix lightly (less than ¹/₂ minute).

On a lightly floured surface, knead gently and briefly (less than ¹/₂ minute) adding more flour if necessary.

Roll out the biscuits to ¹/₄" thick (approx. ²/₃ cm) and cut, using a pastry cutter.

Lay the biscuits on an ungreased baking tray and bake in the preheated oven for 8-10 minutes.

Based on a recipe from Gail Harris of Covelo, California.

POTATO DISHES

HOME FRIES   *Makes 4-6 servings*

Home fries can be prepared in a number of ways but the basic recipe is this: thinly slice potatoes, sauté them until lightly browned, and season with salt and pepper. To liven things up, other ingredients (such as garlic, shallots, onions, peppers, chiles) may be sautéed with the potatoes, and other seasonings may be added (like paprika, parsley).

The variations you can achieve are endless but when there's no margin for error (like when guests are expected), I use the recipe from John Hadamuscin's book, *Enchanted Evenings* -- the sage seems to give this dish a homely flavour that's particularly welcoming. The following is based on his recipe.

Ingredients   ¼ cup olive oil (2 ounces or *60ml*)

                   1 large clove garlic, finely chopped

                   1 small or medium onion, chopped

                   2 lbs. small waxy potatoes, with skins on (*972g*)

                   1 teaspoon rosemary

                   1 tablespoon chopped sage (or ¾ tablespoon dried)

                   salt and pepper to taste

Procedure   Chop the onion and garlic and set aside. Slice the
                   potatoes (don't peel them) and set them aside.

                   In a large frying pan, heat the olive oil. Add the onion
                   and garlic and sauté over medium heat for around 5
                   minutes.

                   Add the potatoes and toss to coat with the oil. Cover
                   and cook, turning frequently, for around 20 minutes.

                   Add the herbs and toss to combine. Continue cooking,
                   turning frequently, until potatoes are well-browned and
                   tender (around 10 more minutes).

                   Season with salt and pepper, and serve.

POTATO KNISHES   *makes around 48 knishes*

I admit these are involved (an optimist would say 'fun') but in the end, they're worth the effort, plus they freeze well so you can put some aside for special occasions. By the way, you can add what you like to the filling -- sautéed mushrooms and/or leeks and/or chiles, etc. Basically, you can put what you like in them provided there's something like potato and egg to hold the filling together.

Ingredients with the original American measurements:

Dough:
  2 cups instant blending flour
  ½ teaspoon baking powder
  ½ cup oil
  ½ cup tepid water
  1 egg, lightly beaten

Filling:
  ½ stick of butter (or, for a kosher recipe, use
      ¼ cup chicken fat or oil)
  1 large onion, chopped
  2 large cloves garlic, chopped
  2 lb. potatoes or mashed potatoes
  (a pot of salted water if starting with raw
      potatoes)
  2 eggs
  ½ tablespoon kosher salt
      (or ¾ teaspoon table salt)
  1 teaspoon pepper

Oil to coat knishes

Ingredients with British measurements (*followed by metric*):

Dough:

½ cup corn flour (around 2½ oz. or *70g*)

1¾ cup plain flour (around 8½ oz. or *240 g*)

½ teaspoon baking powder

4 oz. oil (*120 ml*)

4 oz. tepid water (*120 ml*)

1 egg, lightly beaten

Filling:

2 oz. butter (*55 g*) (or, for a kosher recipe, use chicken fat or oil)

1 large onion, chopped

2 large cloves garlic, chopped

2 lb. potatoes or mashed potatoes (*900 g*)

(a pot of salted water if starting with raw potatoes)

2 eggs

½ tablespoon kosher salt

(or ¾ teaspoon table salt)

1 teaspoon coarsely ground black pepper

Oil to coat knishes

Procedure

For the dough: Combine the flours and baking powder in a bowl. Make a well in the centre and add the oil, water, and beaten egg. Mix thoroughly and knead well. Cover and let stand one hour.

For the filling: Melt the butter (or fat) over medium-high heat in a heavy bottomed skillet or frying pan. Add the onions and garlic and stir as you fry them. After 5 minutes or so, reduce the heat to medium-low. Continue to stir occasionally until everything is lightly browned. (This will take around 10-15 minutes.)

The rolled knish dough with a row of potato filling.

Scoop out the browned onions and garlic and set them aside. Reserve the melted butter (or fat).

(If you are using leftover mashed potato, skip this step.) Boil a quart (*1 litre*) of water containing a half-teaspoon salt. (It isn't necessary to peel the potatoes but if you prefer your potato filling without skins, peel the potatoes now.) Cut up the raw potatoes and add them to the boiling water. Simmer until a fork inserts easily (but before they've turned mushy). Drain the potatoes and mash them.

Add the reserved melted butter (or fat) to the mashed potatoes along with the eggs, salt and pepper, and beat well. Stir in the onions and garlic.

Lightly grease 2 baking sheets.

Sprinkle plenty of flour over a flat working surface. Begin with a third of the dough and knead it again briefly. (You may add more flour to the dough if necessary but the dough should be fairly elastic and oily so don't try to get it to a pastry dough consistency.) With a well-floured rolling pin, roll the dough out to a rectangular shape. Using your fingers,

A row of knishes cut from the dough.

place a row of the potato filling along the long edge of the dough.

Lift up the edge of the dough and pull it over the filling, rolling the filling until it's completely covered with the dough. Use a knife to cut off the filled row of knishes from the remaining dough. Then cut that row of filling into individual knishes, around 2"-3" long (*5-7.5cm*), and set them on the greased baking sheet. Continue filling, rolling, and cutting the remaining knishes until all the ingredients are used up. When you're about 15 minutes from completion, preheat the oven to 175°C or Gas Mark 4 (350°F).

Lightly brush the tops of the knishes with the oil and bake them in the preheated oven for around 30 minutes or until lightly browned.

THANKSGIVING DISHES

CRANBERRY SAUCE   *makes 2 cups (around 16 ounces)*

Cranberry sauce is so quick and easy to make, the only excuse for buying it ready made is if you can't find the berries fresh. And though you might think 16 ounces is a lot to make, cranberry sauce is something that's even devoured by people who aren't aficionados of jams and jellies (like myself). And if you do have leftovers, it's excellent spread in a sandwich.

Ingredients with the original American measurements:
1 cup water
2 cups whole cranberries
1 cup sugar

Ingredients with British measurements (*followed by metric*):

        8 oz. water (*237 ml*)

        ½ lb. whole cranberries (*230 g*)

        ½ lb. sugar (*230 g*)

Procedure   Wash the cranberries and remove any that have gone soft.

                Bring the sugar and water to a boil and simmer for a few minutes.

                Add the cranberries and return to the boil. Reduce heat, cover and simmer for around 10 minutes (or until they stop popping). Skim off the froth if there's alot of it. Let the sauce cool.

                (You may, if you like, add a dash of cognac.)

CREAMED PEAS AND ONIONS   *Yield: four servings*

My memories of Thanksgiving always include turkey, stuffing, and cranberry sauce, but I can't think of one that didn't also include creamed peas and onions. You can use fresh or frozen peas but by the time Thanksgiving rolls around,[16] I think you'll be limited to frozen (and they're fine). This really isn't hard to make -- the worst part is peeling all those little onions.

> Ingredients with the original American measurements:
>
> 2 lbs. fresh peas, still in pods (or 2²/₃ cups frozen)
>
> 1 lb. white baby onions
>
> 1 quart water with 1 teaspoon salt
>
> White sauce: 3 tablespoons butter
>   3 tablespoons flour
>   ¹/₂ teaspoon salt
>   ¹/₈ teaspoon pepper
>   2 cups warmed milk (or half & half)

Ingredients with British measurements (*followed by metric*):

2 lbs. fresh peas, still in pods   (*900 g*)
(or 10 oz. frozen peas [*280 g*])

1 lb. pickling or silverside onions   (*454 g*)

32 oz. water (*1 litre*) with 1 teaspoon salt

white sauce: 1¹/₃ oz. butter   (*40 ml*)
2 heaped tablespoons flour   (*40 g*)
¹/₂ teaspoon salt
¹/₈ teaspoon pepper
16 oz. warmed milk (or equal parts milk and single cream)   (*470 ml*)

---

[16]Most people think Thanksgiving is the last Thursday in November; it's not - it's the 4th Thursday (which is *usually* also the last Thursday).

Procedure   If you're using fresh peas: shell and wash them, and
                reserve a few pea pods along with the shelled peas.

                Cut the ends off the onions and remove the outer skins.
                (Note: It's easier if you first blanch them in boiling
                water for 30 seconds, and then drain and cool them
                before peeling.)

                Fill a pot with water and add the salt. Cover and bring
                to a boil. Add the onions to the boiling water. (If
                you're using fresh peas, add them as well, along with
                the reserved pea pods for extra flavour.) Return to a
                boil and cook uncovered for 5 minutes.

                While this is cooking, start preparing the white sauce
                (recipe below) and warming the milk for it.

                After 5 minutes, reduce the heat under the onions,
                cover, and cook until tender -- a further 3 to 7 minutes
                (if using frozen peas, add them to the simmering onions
                and let the water return to a boil before reducing the
                heat and covering).

                Drain the peas and onions (discarding any pods). Put
                them into a warm serving dish. When the white sauce
                is ready, pour it over the peas and onions, and serve.

                White sauce:

                    Melt the butter in a heavy bottomed skillet or
                    frying pan.

                    Sprinkle in the flour, salt, and pepper and stir to
                    blend. Continue stirring over a low heat until the
                    mixture is smooth.

                    Slowly stir in the warmed milk (or milk/cream
                    mixture) and bring this to a boil. Continue stirring
                    until the sauce has thickened.

                    Pour it over the peas and onions.

Based on a recipe from Middie Sarchioto of Schenectady, New York.

SWEET POTATO AND MARSHMALLOWS   *makes 4 servings*

To find the ingredients for this recipe, you might feel you've been sent
on a treasure hunt. The type of sweet potato this recipe uses is the one
with the bright orange flesh, which sometimes is and sometimes isn't
available in English supermarkets, so check that it's there before buying
the soured cream and marshmallows. For that matter, make sure you
can find the white marshmallows, too.

Ingredients with the original American measurements:
1 pound sweet potatoes or yams (about 3 medium)
½ cup dairy sour cream
1 egg yolk
½ teaspoon salt
¼ teaspoon ground mace
¾ cup miniature white marshmallows

Ingredients with British measurements (*followed by metric*):

> 1 pound sweet potatoes or yams (*454 g*)
>   (about 3 medium)
>
> 5 oz. soured cream (*142 ml*)*
>
> 1 egg yolk
>
> ½ teaspoon salt (or 1 teaspoon kosher salt)
>
> ¼ teaspoon ground mace
>
> 1½ oz. miniature white marshmallows (*43 g*)
>   or enough to cover

---

* If soured cream is unavailable, substitute using 4 oz. yogurt (*120 ml*) mixed
with 1-1/2 tablespoons butter.

Procedure   Wash the sweet potatoes (but don't pare them).

Heat to boiling enough salted water that'll cover the potatoes. *Then* add the potatoes, cover, and return to a boil. Cook until tender (30 to 35 minutes) and drain. Remove the skins and place the sweet potatoes in a large mixing bowl.

Preheat the oven to 180°C or gas mark 4 (350°F).

Mash the sweet potatoes. Combine the sour cream, egg yolk, salt, and mace and add them to the sweet potatoes. Using an electric mixer, beat on medium speed until smooth.

Pour the mixture into a buttered 1-litre casserole dish and top with the marshmallows.

Cook, uncovered, until marshmallows are puffed and golden brown, about 30 minutes.

Based on a recipe from Middie Sarchioto of Schenectady, New York.

SAME NAME, DIFFERENT DISH (LASAGNE)

MUSHROOM AND ONION LASAGNE   *serves 8*

On my first trip to England, I saw lasagne on a pub menu and quickly ordered it. However, when they brought it to my table, I thought surely they'd made a mistake. Most lasagne served in England is primarily a tomato and beef mince mixture, with lasagne noodles, cheddar cheese and *maybe* some mozzarella. It looks and tastes nothing like the lasagne served in the US so it's quite a shock when you first order it. The following recipe is for the type of lasagne served in the US -- it's from my sister, Middie, whose mother-in-law was from Italy and who taught Mid the secrets of her cooking.

Ingredients with the original American measurements:

3 lb. seasoned tomato sauce

11-12 oz. ricotta seasoned with

    2 tablespoons fresh chopped chives

      (or 1 tablespoon dried chives)

    1 teaspoon dried basil

    salt and pepper

½ lb. onions, sliced

1 lb. mushrooms, sliced

¼ cup olive oil (more if needed)

crushed red pepper to taste

1½ lb. mozzarella, shredded

½ lb. Romano, shredded

9 oz. lasagne noodles

for the lasagne water: 3 Tbl. salt and 1 Tbl. olive oil

Ingredients with British measurements (*followed by metric*):

> 3 lb. store-bought seasoned tomato sauce (*1.36 kg*)
> or, if you can't find it, homemade (list follows)
> *For homemade tomato sauce, you'll need:*
> 3 lb. tomatoes, either fresh or tinned (*1.36 kg*)
> 3 cloves of garlic
> a medium onion
> 2 Tbl. olive oil
> 2 oz. dry white wine (*60 ml*)
> 2 Tbl. *double concentrated tomato puree*
> parsley, oregano, and crushed red pepper to taste
> also, salt and pepper to taste

> 11-12 oz. ricotta cheese* (*310-340 g*)
> *seasoned with:*
> 2 Tbl. fresh chopped chives (or 1 Tbl. dried)
> 1 teaspoon dried basil
> crushed red pepper to taste
> salt and pepper

> ½ lb. onions, sliced (*230 g*)

> 1 lb. mushrooms, sliced (*455 g*)

> 2 ounces olive oil (more if needed) (*60 ml*)

> 1½ lb. mozzarella cheese, shredded (*680 g*)

> ½ lb. Romano cheese, shredded (*230 g*)
> (if unavailable, use Parmesan)

> 9 oz. lasagne noodles (*250 g*)

> for the lasagne water: 3 Tbl. salt and 1 Tbl. olive oil

---

* If ricotta is unavailable, you may use paneer instead (recipe on page 213) but you'll need to prepare it a day ahead of time. Alternatively, you may substitute using a dry curd cottage cheese, provided you first wrap it in muslin and squeeze it well.

For this recipe, you will be layering lasagne noodles; a ricotta, mushroom & onion mixture; seasoned tomato sauce; shredded mozzarella; and shredded Romano (or Parmesan) cheese. It is a time consuming dish to prepare so I usually make the ricotta mixture and the tomato sauce the day before.

Procedure   If you're making the tomato sauce from scratch, prepare it now. (If starting with fresh tomatoes, you'll find the skins come off much more easily if you first stick a fork in the stem end and immerse the tomato completely in boiling water for around 12 seconds.)

- Blend (or crush) the tomatoes until no large chunks are left. (A smooth puree is not necessary.)
- Cut the garlic into large pieces and set them aside. Finely chop the onion and set that aside.
- In a large pot, heat the olive oil and sauté the garlic until browned. Next add the onion and sauté it until translucent. Add the wine, stir, and follow with the crushed tomatoes, tomato paste (*double concentrated tomato puree*), and seasonings. Simmer for 1-2 hours, stirring often.

Now, prepare the onions and mushrooms:
- Slice the onions and the mushrooms separately and set each aside.
- Heat 2 tablespoons of the olive oil in a large frying pan over a medium-low heat. Add the onions and sauté slowly, stirring often. Once they begin to brown, remove from the pan and set aside.
- Heat the remaining olive oil and sauté the mushrooms until they've given up their moisture and most of it has evaporated. Combine the mushrooms with the onions and set aside.

Next, prepare the ricotta mixture. Put the ricotta into a large bowl and stir in the following:

- 1 cup (8 oz. or *240 ml*) of the tomato sauce
- all of the sautéed mushrooms and onions
- the seasonings: chopped chives, basil, crushed red pepper, salt and pepper

Shred the mozzarella and the Romano (or Parmesan) separately and set each aside.

Preheat the oven to 160°C or gas mark 3 (325°F) and prepare the lasagne noodles. Note: Although the lasagne noodles sold here *say* 'no pre-cooking required', I find they result in a noodle that's just a bit too *al dente* for me so to get them the way I like, I boil them first (but only for a couple of minutes).

- Fill a large pot with water. Add 3 Tbl. salt and a tablespoon of olive (or other) oil. Bring to a rapid boil and add the lasagne, stirring constantly with a wooden spoon to keep the noodles from sticking. Let it return to a rapid boil and set the timer for 12 minutes (or 2, if using the 'no pre-cooking required' noodles). When the timer goes, check to see if they've softened. If not, boil a bit longer but keep in mind the noodles will continue to cook in the oven. When the noodles are ready, drain them and put them in a bowl of cold salted water.

Spoon some of the tomato sauce into the base of a 9 x 12½ x 2" (*23 x 32 x 5 cm*) pan, and spread it so the bottom is completely covered.

Lay down a layer of the noodles. Cover the noodles with a layer of the ricotta mixture, followed by a layer each of tomato sauce, mozzarella, and Romano. Continue layering in this order until all are used up: noodles - ricotta - tomato sauce - mozzarella - Romano (you should finish with the Romano on top).

Bake in a preheated 160°C or gas mark 3 oven for 1 hour and 10 minutes or until golden brown on top.

COOKIES, BROWNIES, AND SWEET BREADS

CHOCOLATE CHIP COOKIES	*makes approx. 36 cookies*

You can buy packaged chocolate chip cookies in English supermarkets but they tend to be hard, like shortbread biscuits, rather than soft and chewy. For the soft and chewy variety, follow this recipe but be sure to scoop them off the baking sheet when they've barely browned, and not a second after.

Ingredients with the original American measurements:

½ cup softened (*not* melted) butter
¼ cup granulated sugar
½ cup brown sugar, packed
1 egg
½ teaspoon vanilla
½ teaspoon water
1 cup and 2 tablespoons sifted self-rising flour
½ teaspoon baking soda
½ teaspoon salt
1 cup chocolate chips
½ cup chopped walnuts, optional

Ingredients with British measurements (*followed by metric*):

        3½ oz. softened (*not* melted) butter (*100 g*)

        1¾ oz. granulated sugar (*45 g*)

        3½ oz. brown sugar (*100 g*)

        1 egg

        ½ teaspoon vanilla

        ½ teaspoon water

        5 oz. sifted self-raising flour (*140 g*)

        ½ teaspoon baking soda

        ½ teaspoon salt

        6 oz. chocolate chips (*170 g*)

        1¾ oz. chopped walnuts, optional (*45 g*)

Procedure   Note: Remember to allow enough time for the butter to soften before proceeding.

Preheat the oven to 190°C or Gas mark 5 (375°F) and lightly grease two baking sheets.

In a mixing bowl, cream the butter. Add the sugars and beat until creamy. Beat in the egg, vanilla, and water.

Sift and measure the flour. Stir the flour and other dry ingredients into the batter.

Stir in the chocolate chips (and nuts, if using them).

Place the batter by the spoonful onto the greased baking sheets, being sure to allow a good inch (*2.5 cm*) between spoonfuls as they will spread. Bake *just* until light brown around the edges (8-10 minutes). Using a spatula, scoop the cookies onto newspaper to cool -- don't be put off when they 'accordion' as you scoop them; they'll lay fairly flat once they slide off the spatula. Store in an airtight container.

Based on a recipe from Gail Harris of Covelo, California.

BROWNIES	*makes 24 2" x 2" squares (5 x 5cm)*

Some people are pastry people, some people are chocolate people. Pastry people will fare fine in England while those of us who are keen on chocolate are pretty much limited to chocolate bars (not that I'm complaining). But once in awhile, a nice moist brownie would really hit the spot so I've included this recipe for those times. Brownies are a moist and chewy, chocolate cake that's cut into squares; the name 'brownie' is nothing more than a reference to its colour.

Ingredients with the original American measurements:

1 cup butter, softened

1³/₄ cups (packed) light brown sugar

1¹/₂ teaspoons vanilla extract

5 ounces unsweetened chocolate

5 eggs, beaten

1 cup all purpose flour

Optional: 1 cup chopped walnuts

Ingredients with British measurements (*followed by metric*):

10¹/₂ ounces butter, softened   (*300 g*)

12 ounces light brown sugar   (*340 g*)

1¹/₂ teaspoons essence of vanilla

5 eggs, beaten (*medium sized*)

3¹/₂ ounces cocoa powder   (*90 g*)

4 ounces plain flour   (*113 g*)

Optional: 5¹/₃ oz. chopped walnuts (*160 g*)

Procedure

Note: You'll need to allow enough time for the butter to soften before proceeding. Set it somewhere warm enough for it to soften but not melt -- melted butter won't work for this recipe.

Butter the inside of a 9" x 13" (*23 x 33cm*) baking pan. (I save butter wrappers and use them to grease pans, since they come ready-greased.)

Preheat the oven to 175°C or gas mark 4 (350°F).

In a large mixing bowl, cream the butter and sugar.

Add the vanilla and the beaten eggs, and combine using an electric whisk or hand mixer.

Add the cocoa powder and flour and continue beating until evenly mixed.

Add the nuts and stir them in with a spoon.

Pour the mixture into the greased baking pan and bake for 20-30 minutes or until a toothpick inserted in the centre comes out clean. A handy cake-baking tip (and one that also applies to brownies) which I picked up from John Hadamuscin's book *Special Occasions*, is to lay foil loosely over the edges of the cake, if they're starting to dry out before the centre has finished cooking. This way the cake should be moist throughout -- not cracked and dried on the edges.

Once it's ready, lay the baking pan on a cooling rack to cool down. When it's ready, you don't need to remove the cake from the pan, just cut it into squares and serve. It's nice by itself or with a scoop of vanilla ice cream.

BANANA BREAD (CAKE)   *makes one loaf*

Banana bread is a good way to use up over-ripe bananas, and it should only be made with very ripe bananas as they will impart the strongest flavour. If you have some over-ripe bananas but no immediate plans to make banana bread, simply peel the bananas, put them in a plastic bag and freeze them. When you're ready to make the bread, take them out and let them defrost. They'll be brown and mushy but they will make an excellent bread.

There are literally hundreds of banana bread recipes but the best one I have found is the one in Mollie Katzen's *Moosewood Cookbook.* The following recipe is based on hers.

Ingredients with the original American measurements:
1 cup whole wheat flour 1 cup white flour $1/2$ teaspoon salt $1/4$ teaspoon baking soda $1 1/2$ teaspoons baking powder $1/8$ teaspoon nutmeg 1 teaspoon ground cinnamon
$3/4$ cup ripe bananas (2 medium) $1/3$ cup strong black coffee
$1/2$ cup softened butter $2/3$ cup packed brown sugar 1 jumbo egg or 2 small eggs 1 teaspoon vanilla extract $1/4$ teaspoon almond extract $1/2$ teaspoon grated orange rind
sesame seeds and butter to coat pan

The British ingredients and measurements (*followed by metric*) are incorporated into the instructions:

Procedure	Note: You'll need to allow enough time for the butter to soften before proceeding. Set it somewhere warm enough for it to soften but not melt -- melted butter won't work for this recipe.
	Preheat the oven to 175°C or gas mark 4 (350°F).
	This recipe is made by alternately adding a flour mixture and a banana mixture to a butter mixture.
Flour mix	*Sift together twice:*
	4 oz. wholemeal flour (*115 g*)
	4 oz. plain flour (*115 g*)
	½ teaspoon salt
	¼ teaspoon baking soda
	1½ teaspoons baking powder
	⅛ teaspoon nutmeg
	1 teaspoon ground cinnamon
Banana mix	*Puree together or beat well:*
	2 ripe medium-sized bananas
	2⅔ oz. strong black coffee (*80 ml*) -- made from ground coffee, not instant
Butter mix	*Cream together in a large bowl:*
	4 oz. softened butter (*115 g*)
	5 oz. brown sugar (*140 g*)
	Into the butter mixture, beat in the egg (or eggs, one at a time):
	1 large (or extra large) egg, or 2 small eggs

To the butter mixture, add the following and beat until light in colour:

1 teaspoon essence of vanilla

$^1/_8$ teaspoon essence of almond

$^1/_2$ teaspoon grated orange rind

Coating: approx. $1^1/_2$ oz. sesame seeds *(43 g)*

butter to coat pan

To the butter mixture add about a third of the flour mixture and combine gently. Next add half of the banana mixture and combine. Continue adding these mixtures alternately until they are used up, ending with the flour mixture.

Liberally butter the inside of a loaf pan. Pour the sesame seeds into the pan and shake them around to coat the sides (best to do this over a sink).

Pour the mixture into the pan and bake for 40-60 minutes or until a toothpick inserted in the centre comes out clean.

Lay the loaf pan on a cooling rack. After 10 minutes, carefully slide a butter knife along the inside edges of the pan being careful to avoid slicing off the sesame-seeded-crust. Turn the pan upsidedown and tap the loaf free. Leave the banana bread on the cooling rack until cool.

Based on a recipe from Mollie Katzen's *Moosewood Cookbook.*

ZUCCHINI (*COURGETTE*) BREAD (*CAKE*)   *makes two large loaves*

This recipe makes a sweet green-speckled bread (*cake*) which refrigerates and freezes well. It's a good way to use up the excess zucchini (*courgettes*) from an over-productive garden.

Ingredients with the original American measurements:

---

3 eggs, beaten

3 cups all purpose flour

2 cups sugar

1 cup oil

2 cups shredded zucchini

1 teaspoon salt

2 teaspoons vanilla extract

1¹/₄ teaspoons baking soda

¹/₂ teaspoon baking powder

Optional: ¹/₄ cup chopped nuts and/or
            ¹/₄ cup raisins

Ingredients with British measurements (*followed by metric*):

3 eggs, beaten (*medium sized*)

³/₄ lb. self-raising sponge or cake flour (*340 g*)

1 lb. sugar (*454 g*)

8 oz. oil (*240 ml*)

10 oz. shredded *courgettes* (*280 g*)

1 teaspoon salt

2 teaspoons essence of vanilla

Optional: 1¹/₃ oz. chopped nuts (*40 g*) and/or
           2¹/₄ oz. raisins (*65 g*)

Procedure   Preheat the oven to 175°C or gas mark 4 (350°F).

In a large mixing bowl, combine all the ingredients and mix well.

Pour the mixture into two lightly-greased 4½ x 8½" loaf pans* (11.5 x 21.5 cm) and bake for 45-55 minutes or until a toothpick inserted in the centre comes out clean.

Lay the loaf pans on a cooling rack. After 10 minutes, slide a butter knife along the inside edges to free the bread from the sides of the pan. Turn them upsidedown and tap the loaves free. Leave the loaves on the cooling racks until cool.

Based on a recipe from the late Bea Dunn of Newington, Connecticut.

---

* Measure pans across the top from the inside.

PIES, COBBLER, JAM

PIE CRUST	*makes a single crust for a 9" (23 cm) pie plate*

Ingredients with the original American measurements:

1 cup all purpose flour
large pinch of salt
⅓ cup chilled lard
2 tablespoons chilled butter
2+ tablespoons iced water

Ingredients with British measurements (*followed by metric*):

4 oz. plain flour (*115 g*)

large pinch of salt

2¼ oz. chilled lard (*65 g*)

1 oz. chilled butter (*30 g*)

2+ tablespoons iced water (*30-40 ml*)

Procedure   Combine the flour and salt.

Cut the lard and butter into the flour until it has an evenly coarse consistency. Sprinkle the dough with 2 tablespoons of iced water and lightly combine with a fork. If necessary, a bit more iced water may be added until the pastry begins to hold together and can be shaped into a ball.

Form the dough into a ball and cover with plastic wrap (*cling film*). Refrigerate for at least one hour (preferably overnight).

Remove the dough from the refrigerator. Lightly flour a flat surface and starting at the centre of the dough, roll it out to a circle until it is ⅛" thick (⅓ cm).

Carefully and lightly roll the pastry back around the rolling pin itself, position it over your pie plate (*flan dish*), and gently unroll it.

Press the dough into the bottoms and sides and cut off any excess. Refrigerate the pie shell while you make your pie filling.

Baking blind: When pre-baked pie crusts (*baking blind*) are called for, preheat the oven to 220°C or gas mark 7 (425°F). Prick the bottom and sides of the pie crust all over with a fork and place in the preheated oven. After 5 minutes or so, check to see if there's any swelling; if so, press it down gently. Check for swelling again in 5 more minutes. Bake for a total of around 15-20 minutes or until golden. Cool on a wire rack.

PECAN PIE   *one 9"* (23 cm) *pie*

This pie is great with a scoop of vanilla ice cream on it (or on its own).
If you can't find (or afford) pecans, use walnuts -- they'll do fine.

Ingredients with the original American measurements:
one 9" (*23 cm*) pie crust
3 eggs
1 cup sugar
1 cup corn syrup (light or dark or combination)
⅓ cup melted butter
1 teaspoon vanilla extract
½ teaspoon salt
1½ cups pecan halves

Ingredients with British measurements (*followed by metric*):

    one 9" (*23 cm*) pie crust (recipe on page 186)

    2¼ oz. melted butter (*60 g*)

    7½ oz. (¾ cup) glucose syrup (*225g*)

    1 tablespoon just-boiled (or very hot) water

    1 tablespoon treacle, optional

    3 eggs (*medium sized*)

    6 oz. sugar (*170 g*)*

    1 teaspoon essence of vanilla

    ½ teaspoon salt

    6 oz. pecan halves (*170 g*)

---

* This equals 3/4 cup of sugar and not a whole cup as called for in the
American ingredients box. Since glucose syrup is about twice as sweet as
corn syrup, I've adjusted the amounts of sugar and syrup called for in the
British ingredients.

Procedure   Prepare a pie crust and let it chill 1 hour.

Preheat the oven to 230°C or Gas mark 8 (450°F). When the dough has chilled, roll it out and line a lightly-greased 9" (*23cm*) pie plate with it. Prick the bottom and sides of the pie crust all over with a fork and bake for 5 minutes. Let it cool on a wire rack.

Lower the oven heat to 190°C or gas mark 5 (375°F) and proceed to make the filling.

Melt the butter. Pour it into a large mixing bowl along with the glucose syrup,* the very hot water, and the treacle (if you're using it). Stir until the mixture is thoroughly combined. Add the remaining ingredients (except the pecans) and stir. Beat well with an electric mixer.

Now add the pecans and stir to mix.

Pour the filling into the prepared pie crust and bake 40-50 minutes or until a knife inserted halfway between the edge and the centre of the pie comes out clean.

PUMPKIN PIE   *makes a single 9" (23 cm) pie*

Pumpkin pie recipes say to use fresh or canned pumpkin, but if you've ever made it with fresh, you'll know there's a big difference. This is one of those rare instances where canned is actually preferable to fresh for the simple reason that it's next to impossible to get the fresh puree as thick as the canned. So, if you can't find the tins but you can find fresh acorn squash or pumpkin, make your puree as thick as possible. And if you can find the tins, stock up.

---

* You may need to run the jar of glucose syrup under hot water first to loosen it, as it's impossibly viscous.

Ingredients with the original American measurements:

one 9" (*23 cm*) unbaked pie crust

2 cups canned pumpkin or fresh, cooked pumpkin

$^2/_3$ cup brown sugar

$^1/_2$ teaspoon salt

1 teaspoon ground cinnamon

$^1/_2$ teaspoon ground ginger

$^1/_4$ teaspoon nutmeg or allspice

$^1/_8$ teaspoon cloves

1 cup milk or heavy cream

2 eggs, lightly beaten

$^1/_4$ cup brandy

1 tablespoon melted butter

Ingredients with British measurements (*followed by metric*):

one 9" (*23 cm*) unbaked pie crust

1 lb. tinned pumpkin   (*454 g*)
    (or use fresh pumpkin or acorn squash puree,*
    along with 1 tablespoon cornstarch dissolved in
    1 tablespoon of water)

$4^3/_4$ oz. brown sugar (*135 g*)

$^1/_2$ teaspoon salt (or 1 teaspoon kosher salt)

1 teaspoon ground cinnamon

$^1/_2$ teaspoon ground ginger

$^1/_4$ teaspoon nutmeg or allspice

$^1/_8$ teaspoon cloves

---

* The recipe for puree is on page 215. Note: acorn squash makes for a more solid puree.

8 oz. milk or single cream** (*237 ml*)

2 eggs, lightly beaten

2 oz. brandy (*60 ml*)

1 tablespoon melted butter (*15 ml*)

Procedure   Prepare a pie crust (see recipe on page 186).

Preheat the oven to 230°C or gas mark 8 (450°F).

In a large mixing bowl, combine the dry ingredients with the pumpkin. Add the remaining ingredients and beat with an electric mixer.

Pour the filling into the unbaked pie crust. Bake in the preheated oven for 15 minutes and then reduce the heat to 175°C or gas mark 4 (350°F) and bake for a further 50 minutes (or until a knife inserted in the centre comes out clean).

Allow the pie to cool.

Serve with sweetened whipped cream.

** If you're using homemade pumpkin puree, then use extra thick single cream or else whipping cream instead of the milk -- the homemade puree is never as solid as the tinned.

PEACH COBBLER (OR ANY FRUIT, REALLY)

Cobblers can be made with virtually any fruit so why not make it with
what's in season? (Blackberry cobbler is especially nice.)

Ingredients with the original American measurements:

For fruit mixture:

    4 cups sliced skinned peaches (or other fruit)

    $^1/_3$ cup sugar

    1 tablespoon all purpose flour

    2 (or more) tablespoons butter

    $^3/_4$ teaspoon cinnamon

For dough:

    $1^1/_2$ cups sifted all-purpose flour

    1 tablespoon baking powder

    $^1/_4$ teaspoon salt

    3 tablespoons butter

    around $^1/_2$ cup milk

Ingredients with British measurements (*followed by metric*):

    For fruit mixture:

        1 lb., 5 oz. sliced skinned peaches
            or other fruit (*600 g*)

        $2^1/_2$ oz. sugar (*75 g*)

        1 tablespoon plain flour

        2 (or more) tablespoons butter (*30 ml*)

        $^3/_4$ teaspoon cinnamon

    For dough:

        6 oz. sifted plain flour (*170 g*)

        1 tablespoon baking powder

¹/₄ teaspoon salt

3 tablespoons butter (*45 ml*)

around 4 oz. milk (*120 ml*)

Procedure   Preheat the oven to 220°C or Gas mark 7 (425°F).

In a large saucepan, combine the sliced peaches, flour and sugar. Over a low heat, bring them to a boil, stirring often. Continue cooking until the fruit is tender (around 5 minutes).

Pour the fruit mixture into an 8" sq. baking dish (*20 cm*). Dot this with the butter and sprinkle the cinnamon over it.

Sift and measure the flour. In a mixing bowl combine the flour, baking powder and salt. Using your fingertips, pinch in the butter until the dough has an evenly coarse consistency. Stir the milk in with a fork until the dough is free from the sides of the bowl.

Put the dough on a lightly floured surface and knead it briefly (less than half a minute). Using a rolling pin, roll the dough to about 9" sq. (*23 cm*) and ¹/₂" thick (*1.3 cm*). Place the dough on top of the peaches and press it to the sides of the baking dish.

Bake in a preheated oven for 20-25 minutes or until nicely browned on top. Serve with milk or cream.

APPLE BUTTER   *makes approx. 24 oz.*

Apple butter has no butter in it; 'butter' in this case simply means a thick puree. Although apple butter is nice spread on toast, it's especially nice on a Digestive biscuit with a slice of cheddar on top (thanks to Clare for that discovery).

Ingredients with the original American measurements:

2 lb. well-flavoured cooking apples

1 cup water and/or cider vinegar

approx. 1½ cups white or brown sugar

spices: ½ teaspoon ground cinnamon

            ¼ teaspoon ground cloves

            ⅛ teaspoon ground allspice

1 lemon, optional

Ingredients

2 lb. well-flavoured cooking apples *(900 g)*

8 oz. water and/or cider vinegar *(240 ml)*

approx. 12 oz. white or brown sugar *(340 g)*

spices: ½ teaspoon ground cinnamon
            ¼ teaspoon ground cloves
            ⅛ teaspoon ground allspice

1 lemon, optional

Procedure

Note: You'll need sterilised glass jars and lids.

To sterilise jars and lids:

Put clean jars and lids in a large pot and fill it with water. Bring it to a boil and let it simmer for 15 minutes. Remove the jars and lids, let them drain, and then fill them with the apple butter.

To make the apple butter:

Wash apples, remove stems, and cut into quarters.

In a large pot, bring the water and/or vinegar to a boil. Add the apples and simmer, covered, until soft (around ½ hour).

Put the apples through a strainer or food mill and measure the pulp. For each cup of pulp, add ½ cup sugar (4 oz. or *110 g*). Return the pulp and sugar to the pot and mix.

Stir in the spices.

(If using a lemon, grate the rind and squeeze the lemon. Add the juice and grated rind to your mixture.)

Cook uncovered over low heat stirring constantly until sugar is dissolved. Continue cooking until mixture thickens (or until the point when a small amount of the apple butter put on a plate no longer has a rim of liquid around it).

Pour the apple butter into the hot sterilised jars and seal shut. Label and date the apple butter, and store them on a shelf. Refrigerate after opening.

ICE CREAM AND CUSTARD,
PEANUT BUTTER CHOCOLATES, SNACKS

BANANA SPLIT   *serves one*

This is one of those things you always think you know how to make
until you actually go to make it. After all, when was the last time *you*
had a banana split? So, if you've forgotten, here it is.

Ingredients   one banana

                   3 scoops dairy ice cream (not soft-scoop)

                   chocolate (or fruit) sauce

                   whipped cream

                   chopped nuts (e.g., walnuts)

                   Maraschino cherry
                       (*cocktail cherry with Maraschino flavouring*)

Procedure   Peel the banana and cut it in half lengthwise. Place the
                   two halves side by side in a long serving dish or bowl.

                   Lay the scoops of ice cream along the length of the
                   split banana and generously drizzle with the sauce.

                   Add a dollop or more of whipped cream and sprinkle
                   liberally with chopped nuts. Top with a single cherry.

PEANUT BUTTER ICE CREAM PIE   *one 9" pie* (23 cm)

I do not know the origin of this recipe. I received my copy from my
sister, Leah, but she was at least two people (and many states) away
from the originator. My apologies to the creator of this recipe for not
crediting them. If you try this, you'll see why it's travelled so far.

> Ingredients with the original American measurements:
>
> 9" graham cracker crust, chilled
> 1 quart vanilla ice cream, softened
> ½ cup corn syrup
> ⅓ cup chunky peanut butter

Ingredients with British measurements (*followed by metric*):

> 9" mock graham cracker crust, chilled (*23 cm*)
>   (see recipe on page 213)
> *1 litre* luxury vanilla dairy ice cream,* softened
> 2½ oz. (¼ cup) glucose syrup (*75 ml*)
> 2 tablespoons just-boiled or very hot water
> 3 oz. (⅓ cup) chunky peanut butter (*80 g*)

Procedure   Press half the softened ice cream into the prepared pie crust.

In a small mixing bowl, stir together the glucose syrup and the just-boiled water (you may need to run the jar of glucose syrup under a hot water tap first to loosen it). Once this mixture is thoroughly combined and no longer viscous, stir in the peanut butter.

Pour half of the peanut butter mixture over the ice cream. Cover that with the remainder of the softened ice cream and pour the rest of the peanut butter mixture on top of that.

Freeze the pie until firm -- about 5 hours.

Before cutting the pie, let it stand at room temperature 5 minutes. Use a hot knife to cut, if necessary.

*Use an ice cream that does not have a great deal of air whipped into it (avoid 'soft-scoop' ice cream). Many supermarkets' own brand *luxury dairy* ice creams are fine.

JUNKET RENNET CUSTARD   *makes four servings*

The word custard brings to mind a thick, almost stodgy dessert but this
does not apply to junket rennet custard. It is a very thin custard, one
that makes for a nice light dessert rather than a leaden one, and it is one
I remember fondly from my childhood in the 1950s. I think it is
disappearing now in the US which is a shame because it really is a
simple and refreshing way to complete a meal.

Ingredients with the original American measurements:

1 quart milk

¼ cup sugar

1 teaspoon vanilla extract

1 tablespoon liquid rennet (or 1 junket tablet)

a few drops of food coloring, optional

powdered cinnamon or nutmeg

Ingredients with British measurements (*followed by metric*):

    33 oz. milk (*945 ml*)

    1 tablespoon essence of rennet (*15 ml*)

    up to 2 oz. sugar (*50 g*)

    1 teaspoon essence of vanilla

    a few drops of food colouring, optional

    ground cinnamon or nutmeg

Procedure   Note: These are the directions for making rennet
    custard using *essence of rennet*; you don't need
    directions if you've got a box of Junket Rennet
    Custard, as those directions are on the box.

Heat the milk just to body temperature -- *do not boil it.* (If the milk does boil, let it cool to body temperature before proceeding.)

Add the remaining ingredients (except the cinnamon or nutmeg) to the milk and stir until the sugar is dissolved.

Pour into a glass bowl or individual dishes and leave in a warm spot to set. Once they've set, refrigerate them. When the custards have cooled, sprinkle them with the cinnamon or nutmeg, and serve.

PEANUT BUTTER FUDGE   *makes 1½ lbs. (680 g)*

This is one of those recipes you read twice because you can't believe that's all there is to it. But believe me, the end result won't give you away. It'll taste like you spent hours making it.

Ingredients with the original American measurements:
2 cups chocolate chips
1½ cups peanut butter
1 14-oz. can of sweetened condensed milk
wax paper

Ingredients with British measurements (*followed by metric*):

12 oz. plain (not milk) chocolate chips (*340 g*)

12 oz. peanut butter (*340 g*)

397 g (or *405 g*) tin of sweetened condensed milk

baking parchment

Note: A double boiler is called for in this recipe.

Procedure   In the top of a double boiler, melt the chocolate and peanut butter.

While this is melting, line an 8" x 8" pan (*20 x 20 cm*) with baking parchment.

When the chocolate and peanut butter have melted, remove them from the heat and stir in the condensed milk.

Pour the fudge mixture into the parchment-lined pan.

Chill until firm. Cut into 1" pieces.

Based on a recipe from Leah Ryel of Hendersonville, North Carolina.

PEANUT BUTTER PATTIES   *makes 38-40 patties*

There are certain chocolate bars and sweets you can get in the US but not here (e.g., Peppermint Patties). When I first got this recipe, you couldn't buy Reese's Peanut Butter Cups in England. Now, of course, you can but it's still worth the bother (and I'll be honest, it *is* a bother) to make these as they really do taste that much better than the store-bought ones. And you may as well double the recipe -- they don't last.

Ingredients with the original American measurements:
½ cup butter, softened
1 cup peanut butter
½ lb. confectioners sugar
1 teaspoon salt
1 Hershey bar
wax paper

Above: Coating the peanut butter patties with chocolate.
Below: The coated patties with an old 50p piece for size reference.

Ingredients with British measurements (*followed by metric*):

> 4 oz. butter, softened (*115 g*)
>
> 8½ oz. peanut butter (*240 g*)
>
> ½ lb. icing sugar (*230 g*)
>
> 1 teaspoon salt
>
> *400 g* bar of milk chocolate
>   (e.g., Cadbury's Dairy Milk)
>
> baking parchment

Note: A double boiler is needed for this recipe.

Procedure   In a large mixing bowl, cream the butter. Then add the peanut butter and cream that in. Sift the salt and sugar onto the peanut butter mixture and stir to combine. Roll the mixture into balls and flatten each into 1"-2" wide patties (*2.5-5cm*), around ³/₈" (*1 cm*) thick. Lay the peanut butter patties on a baking parchment-lined baking sheet or tray, and chill at least one hour.

Once the patties have chilled, melt the chocolate in the top of a double boiler. (When it's melted, make sure you won't be disturbed for the next 20 minutes or so because your fingers will be coated in chocolate.) Remove the double boiler from the stove (*hob*) and when the melted chocolate is cool enough to touch (but only just -- you don't want the chocolate to solidify again), thoroughly coat each patty generously with the chocolate. Lay the chocolate-coated patties on the baking parchment and put in the fridge to chill until the chocolate has hardened. Keep these cool until ready to eat.

Based on a recipe from Leah Ryel of Hendersonville, North Carolina (whose recipe was based on one from the *Amish Way Cookbook*).

POPCORN	*makes one litre popped*

I can't understand why popcorn sells in England because the only times I've gotten it, it's been doused in salt or else sweet (which to me makes as much sense as spreading golden syrup on mashed potatoes). For people like me who simply want buttered and *lightly* salted popcorn, here's how to do it. It's easy to make and the key is to keep shaking the pan once the kernels start popping -- if you leave it, they *will* burn.

Ingredients with the original American measurements:

1 tablespoon oil
½ cup popcorn kernels*
2 tablespoons butter
salt to taste

Ingredients with British measurements (*followed by metric*):

1 tablespoon oil (*15 ml*)
3½ oz. popcorn kernels* (*90 g*)
1 oz. butter (*28 g*)
salt to taste

Note: A large (~4 litre) lightweight pot with a tight-fitting lid is needed for this recipe.

Procedure	Coat the bottom of the pot with the oil. Scatter in a few popcorn kernels, cover, and heat on high.
	Meanwhile, melt the butter in a small pan (or in the microwave) and set aside.

---

* Keep popcorn kernels fresh by storing them in an airtight container in the refrigerator.

When the first kernel pops, add the remaining popcorn and quickly replace the lid. Wearing oven gloves, shake the pot back and forth over the heat, keeping the lid in place. Continue shaking the pot over the high heat until the popping subsides.

Remove from heat, keeping the lid on a minute or two to catch any late poppers. Pour the melted butter over the popcorn, sprinkle with salt, mix and eat.

RICE KRISPIES TREATS   *makes 24 squares, 2" x 2" (5 cm x 5 cm)*

This is one of those recipes we've all clipped from the cereal box but, especially after a few house moves, has disappeared. Kellogg's have kindly granted permission to reprint the recipe here.

Ingredients with the original American measurements:
¼ cup butter or margarine
about 40 regular white marshmallows (10 oz.)
or 4 cups miniature marshmallows
6 cups **Kellogg's® Rice Krispies®** cereal

Ingredients with British measurements (*followed by metric*):

2 oz. butter or margarine (*60 ml*)

about 40 regular white marshmallows
or 10 oz. miniature marshmallows (*285 g*)

5¼ oz. **Kellogg's® Rice Krispies®** cereal (*145 g*)

Procedure   Melt the butter in a large saucepan over low heat. Add the marshmallows and stir until completely melted. Remove from heat.

Add **Rice Krispies®** cereal. Stir until well-coated.

Using a buttered spatula (or wax paper [*baking parchment*]), press mixture evenly into buttered 13 x 9 x 2" pan (*33 x 23 x 5 cm*).
Cut into squares when cool.

NOTE: Use fresh marshmallows for best results.

DRINKS

CHOCOLATE EGG CREAM *makes 1 tall glass*

There's no egg in it and there's no cream in it but there is chocolate. It's just called an egg cream because (when it's made right) a foamy head forms that looks like whipped egg whites. You may not be able to create the same remarkable egg-white type of head with bottled *fizzy water* but it will still taste just as refreshing.

> Ingredients with the original American measurements:
>
> 3 tablespoons Fox's u-bet Chocolate Flavor Syrup
> 3 tablespoons ice-cold milk
> fill to top with seltzer

Ingredients with British measurements (*followed by metric*):

3 tablespoons chocolate syrup (1½ ounces or *45 ml)*
3 tablespoons ice-cold milk (1½ ounces or *45 ml)*
fill to top with fizzy water

Procedure These are normally made in tall soda fountain glasses but a British pint glass will do fine.

Into a tall glass, pour the chocolate syrup and the milk, and stir to blend. Continue stirring as you quickly pour in the *fizzy water*. The egg-white-like head is created by the way the seltzer is added (a fast jet of seltzer [*carbonated water*] is deflected off a spoon as the drink is stirred). Using bottled *fizzy water*, you may not be able to create such a fluffy head but don't worry -- it will taste just as good.

ICED COFFEE   *makes 4 tall glasses*

Some places *say* they serve iced coffee, but in reality what they serve is hot coffee filled with ice -- that's diluted coffee. Iced coffee is double-strength brewed coffee that's been chilled and topped up with ice. Aside from its taste, the thing I like best about iced coffee is watching the marble effect created by the half & half as it slowly swirls to the bottom (milk won't create this effect, but a mix of equal parts milk and *single cream* will).

Ingredients with the original American measurements:
1 quart water ½ cup ground coffee half and half (or whole milk) to taste sugar to taste, optional ice

Ingredients with British measurements (*followed by metric*):

32 oz. water
(or *1 litre* -- a few ounces off doesn't matter here)

2 ounces ground coffee (*60g*)

half cream (or a mix of equal parts milk and *single cream*), to taste

sugar to taste, optional

ice

Procedure   Using a drip or immersion coffee maker, prepare coffee as you normally would, but using *double* the amount of coffee (if you don't normally make coffee, then go by the amounts listed above). Note: Do not use a percolator to make iced coffee; percolated coffee is too bitter.

For sweet coffee, add and dissolve the sugar now while the coffee is still hot.

Once the coffee has cooled to room temperature, cover it and place it in the fridge to chill.

When chilled, fill tall glasses with ice. Add the coffee, pour in the cream (or cream mixture) and serve. If the coffee is strong and cold enough, the cream will create the swirling marble effect I mentioned above.

Note: For an iced Irish coffee, add one shot (1½ oz. or *45 ml*) of Bailey's Irish Cream.

ICED TEA   *makes approx. one quart or one litre*[*]

You may be surprised to learn that 50% of Americans drink tea but you'll be less surprised when you find that 80% of that tea is served iced. Some things have pretty much stayed put in their country of origin and iced tea is one of them -- it rubs the British psyche the wrong way (maybe because it never stays hot here long enough for people to want it). This recipe is included for those of us who associate the smell of tea with summer rather than the chill of winter.

Ingredients with the original American measurements:
water to fill a large teapot (approx. 1 quart) ½ cup sugar 3 - 4 strong teabags 1 lemon, optional

---

[*] To make more or less than this amount, allow 1 tablespoon sugar and 1 teaspoon loose tea for each 8 ounce (*230 ml*) glass.

Ingredients with British measurements (*followed by metric*):

> water to fill a large teapot (*approx. 1 litre*)
>
> 4 oz. sugar (*110 g*)
>
> 3 - 4 strong teabags
>
> 1 lemon, optional

Procedure   Place the tea in a large teapot. Boil enough water to fill the pot. Pour the boiling water in up to the top, cover, and let it brew for 5-10 minutes.

When the tea is brewed, give it a good stir and remove the bags. Add the sugar and stir to dissolve. When the tea has reached room temperature, chill it. (In the summer, I usually make a pot in the morning, have hot tea with breakfast, and then ice what's leftover.)

Once chilled, fill tall glasses with ice. If you're using lemon, then squeeze and drop an eighth of a lemon into each glass. Fill the glasses to the brim with the chilled tea, and serve.

LEMONADE (HOMEMADE)   *makes 7 to 8 8-oz. glasses*

Lemonade (what the British refer to as 'homemade lemonade') is readily available in the US and is even sold in frozen concentrated form, but not so here. The only lemonade readily available here is the clear, lemon-flavoured soft drink. Occasionally, though, you can buy boxes of *homemade lemonade* or *traditional style lemon crush* but if you can't find these, or if you just want fresh lemonade, here's what to do:

Ingredients with the original American measurements:
1½ cups water 1¼ cups sugar enough lemons to yield a generous ½ cup of juice

Ingredients with British measurements (*followed by metric*):

> 12 oz. water (*355 ml*)
>
> 10 oz. sugar (*280 g*)
>
> enough lemons to yield at least 4 oz. juice (*120 ml*)
>   (usually around 2 to 3 lemons)

Procedure   In a saucepan, combine the water and sugar and bring
                 to a boil. Continue boiling until the sugar has
                 dissolved. Turn off the heat and let the syrup cool.

                 Squeeze the lemons and add their juice to the cooled
                 syrup to make a lemonade concentrate.

                 (At this point, the concentrate may be frozen. When
                 ready to use, defrost the concentrate and proceed with
                 the next step.)

                 Mix one part concentrate to 1½ parts cold water,
                 leaving enough room for ice. Stir.

SUBSTITUTES FOR HARD-TO-FIND INGREDIENTS

BUTTER FROSTING

When I was growing up, most birthday cakes were iced with butter frosting or boiled frosting. You can buy ready-made butter frosting in the US but you can't always find the ready-made equivalent (called *soft icing*) here. You might say it's sour grapes but I prefer the homemade frosting anyway.

Ingredients with the original American measurements:
½ cup *softened* butter
1 box confectioners sugar
4 tablespoons milk (or 3 tablespoons milk with 1 tablespoon rum or brandy)
2 teaspoons vanilla

Ingredients with British measurements (*followed by metric*):

4 oz. *softened* butter   (*120 ml*)

1 lb. icing sugar   (*454 g*)

4 tablespoons milk (or 3 tablespoons milk with 1 tablespoon rum or brandy)

2 teaspoons vanilla   (*10 ml*)

Procedure   Cream the butter.

Stir in the sugar and cream them together, adding the milk one tablespoon at a time.

Add the vanilla (and rum or brandy, if you're including them) and mix completely.

Using knife or spatula, spread on a cooled cake.

Based on a recipe from Gail Harris of Covelo, California.

CHICKEN BROTH

You can buy chicken stock cubes in England (e.g., 'Just Bouillon' or Knorr's) but I've never seen canned chicken broth here, and many American recipes call for it by the can. So what I do is this: from the poulterer on the market, I buy stripped chicken carcasses (they're very cheap) and make a few batches of chicken broth at a time. I then freeze the broth in plastic yogurt (or other) pots and later, when I need it, just pop out the frozen broth and melt it in a pan. If your freezer is small, you could boil the broth for a longer period of time, making it more concentrated, and freeze your 'concentrate' in ice cube trays.

Ingredients
- 1 chicken carcass
- water, enough to cover carcass completely
- 1 large unpeeled onion, quartered
- 2 stalks celery with leaves, roughly chopped
- 1 large unpeeled carrot, thickly sliced
- 1 large clove unpeeled garlic, crushed
- 1 well-washed leek, sliced (optional)
- 1 teaspoon salt
- 2 teaspoons dried parsley (or 6 sprigs fresh)
- ½ teaspoon thyme
- 1 bay leaf
- 6 peppercorns

Procedure

Combine ingredients in a large pot and bring to a boil.

Simmer, partially covered, for 2-3 hours (the longer the better).

Strain through cheesecloth (*muslin*) into a large bowl. Once cooled, skim off any fat. Pour into containers and date and label them. Freeze for later use in recipes.

Based on a recipe from Karen Muranaka, Boise, Idaho.

(MOCK) GRAHAM CRACKER CRUST   *one 9" (23 cm) pie*

I'll never forget the first time I went looking for a prepared graham cracker crust here -- on that same shopping list, I had Q-tips; cheesecloth; corn starch (I knew that was called something different but had forgotten what it was); and corn syrup -- it wasn't my day. Eventually I learned that Digestive biscuits (which we don't have in the US) can normally be substituted for graham crackers when they're called for in recipes, and that goes for making this crust as well.

Ingredients	6 oz. Digestive biscuits, crushed *(170 g)*
	2½ oz. butter, melted *(70 g)*
Procedure	Lightly grease a 9" pie plate with butter.
	Melt the butter and let it cool slightly.
	Add the crushed biscuits to the butter and stir to blend well.
	Scrape the mixture into the pie plate and press it into the base and up along the sides until all is covered.
	Chill the crust ½ hour or until firm.

PANEER (SUBSTITUTE FOR RICOTTA CHEESE)

If you've a recipe that calls for ricotta cheese and you can't find any, you can either buy plain cottage cheese and hang it in cheesecloth (*muslin*) overnight to drain, or you can make paneer. This recipe for paneer is based on the instructions given in Julie Sahni's *Classic Indian Cooking*.

Ingredients with the original American measurements:
2 quarts of milk
10 oz. yogurt

Ingredients with British measurements (*followed by metric*):

> 64 ounces of milk or around 3½ English pints
> (*approx. 2 litres*)
>
> half-pint (English) of yogurt (*285 ml*)

Note: Cheesecloth (*muslin*) is needed to make this cheese.

Procedure   Line a colander with muslin and place it in the sink.

Bring the milk to a boil in a heavy-bottomed saucepan, stirring often.

Reduce the heat and add the yogurt as the starter. Stir *gently* for ½ minute to one minute until the curd separates from the greenish whey -- the curd should be in lumps, not in tiny pieces.

Pour the curds and whey through the muslin-lined colander. (The whey may be saved and used as the starter for the next batch provided it is made within the next 24 hours.) Gently run cold water over the curds for around 10 seconds. Gather up the corners of the muslin and lightly twist them to squeeze out as much moisture as possible. Tie a string around the loose muslin just above the ball of cheese and hang it to drain for 1½ hours.

Once it's drained, you'll have a crumbly, somewhat moist cheese which in India is called *chenna*.

Place the muslin-covered *chenna* on a clean, flat surface and compress it by leaving a weight on it for half an hour. (A pot filled with tinned baked beans makes for a good weight.)

Once it's compressed, the paneer is ready to use. It will keep for up to 4 days in the refrigerator. (Similarly, ricotta cheese has a short shelf-life.)

Based on the instructions in Julie Sahni's *Classic Indian Cooking.*

PUMPKIN OR ACORN SQUASH PUREE

Tinned pumpkin, fresh pumpkin, and acorn squash are all available in England but never, it seems, when you need them. So, to avoid being caught out at Thanksgiving time, pick up fresh acorn squash or pumpkin, make some puree, and freeze it.

Procedure   Preheat the oven to 160°C or Gas Mark 3 (325°F).

Wash the pumpkin or squash and cut them in two horizontally.

Remove the seeds and membranes and place the halves, cut sides down, on a baking sheet.

Bake in the preheated oven for 1 hour or more, until they're tender and falling apart. Allow them to cool.

If using squash:
Scoop the pulp from the skin and mash it.

If using pumpkin:
Cut it into manageable strips. Slide a knife along each strip of pumpkin (very close to its skin), and lift off the pulp. Put the strips of pulp in a colander to drain (overnight, preferably). Once it's drained, put it through a food mill or else puree it in a blender.

The pumpkin or squash is now ready to use in pumpkin pie or pumpkin soup recipes.

(At this point you may freeze the pumpkin or squash puree for use in recipes later.)

USEFUL INFORMATION

NOTES ON LIVING IN ENGLAND

Ale

Originally, ale differed from beer in that it was not flavoured with hops. Today, however, there is no distinct difference and the terms are virtually synonymous (although lager, stout, porter, etc., would not be referred to as *ale*).

Beer

Types of beer:
Nowadays, with the advent of micro-breweries in the US, Americans are learning there's more to beer than just lager, but for the uninitiated, here are the main British players: *Bitter* - most British beer is *bitter*, a well-hopped beer with a medium to high gravity. *Bitter* is also known as India Pale Ale (IPA), a style of beer which originated in Burton upon Trent for the India trade. *Lager* - most American beers are lagers, a beer produced by bottom fermentation and originating from Bohemia and Bavaria. *Lager* is usually (though not always) lighter in colour than *bitter*. *Mild* - this is an ale with a low gravity (normally in the 3% ABV range)* which is usually darker than bitter (and, I find, tastes slightly sweeter). *Stout* - this very dark beer (blackish-brown in colour) is brewed from roasted malt and unmalted roasted barley, and usually has a high hop rate. All of the aforementioned are available in pubs as well as from off-licences, corner shops and supermarkets. By the way, real ale (cask-

---

* Alcohol by volume

conditioned draught beer) should be served at 12-13°C (around 55°F); I am currently writing in a room that's 11°C and it is *not* warm so let's quash the warm beer myth once and for all.

Pub price vs supermarket price:
In England, the price paid for a pint in the pub is not *significantly* greater than the price paid for a beer from the supermarket. A pub-bought beer in England generally costs around the same as *one and a half* cans of beer from the supermarket. This is not the case in the US where a beer in a bar (or restaurant) often costs the same as *three* beers from the grocery store. (See *pubs.*)

Cheese

The varieties of cheese produced in the British Isles would not fit in one book, let alone one entry, but what I can cover here are two terms which may be unfamiliar to Americans: *Farmhouse cheese* and *fromage frais*.
Loosely speaking, *farmhouse cheese* is cheese which is produced using traditional methods (as opposed to factory-produced cheese). Strictly speaking, farmhouse cheese is any cheese produced by a member of the Farmhouse Cheesemakers Ltd co-operative, as identified by their Farmhouse logo. This co-operative is committed to producing cheese by traditional methods, on farms using their own milk. Farmhouse cheese is widely available and, for the difference in flavour, well worth seeking out. (NB Farmhouse cheese is in no way related to the cheese known in America as 'farmer cheese'. Farmer cheese is simply a pressed form of cottage cheese.)

Fromage frais: Though technically a soft fresh cheese, most people associate *fromage frais* with yogurt: it looks like yogurt, is packaged like yogurt, is sold right alongside it, and, like yogurt, is low in calories. However, unlike yogurt, it does not have that slightly sour taste and so, can often be used in place of (or in addition to) various creams when cooking. The average fat content of *fromage frais* is around 7 or 8%; there is also a 'very low fat' *fromage frais* whose average fat content is just 0.2%.

Electric plugs   It was not until the mid-1990s that *leads* (cords, US) of electrical appliances were required to come equipped with a plug.[17] This was due to the fact that in the past, electricity was controlled by individual boroughs and as a result, there was more than one type of plug.

Electrical outlets   Electrical outlets (or electrical sockets) are called *electrical points* in England. In the US, electrical outlets are normally live at all times. In England, however, most *electrical points* have an on/off switch so this, as well as the on/off switch on the appliance itself, must be turned on for the appliance to work. (However, some electrical appliances have no on/off switch, so they can only be turned on at the *electrical point*.)

The Market Place   Many towns in England have a certain day or days of the week designated 'market day(s)', in which stalls are erected in the town centre

---

[17]There are exceptions to this but usually these are appliances which would be directly wired into a wall (e.g., a cooker).

(usually outdoors) for vendors to sell their goods (which nowadays can range from produce to panties). The merchants are usually from the local area and bring their fish, cheese, etc. to the market to sell. Whereas supermarkets provide a wider variety of foods to choose from, much of what the market place provides is locally-grown and so, having travelled less far, is usually fresher and less expensive than that from the supermarket. Unfortunately, today's hurried lifestyle has forced many into shopping solely at the supermarket (for the convenience of one-stop shopping) but markets have been held for over 1,000 years and once they're gone, they're gone. The market place provides personalised service and advice and, as in your local pub, a sense of community (rather than anonymity) prevails. In the US, town centres have virtually disappeared; it would be a shame to see that happen here.

Off-licences

Off licences are shops that sell alcohol intended for consumption off the premises (as opposed to pubs).

Pubs and pub hours

Formerly, pubs were affiliated with a single brewer so, for a Bass beer, you'd go to a Bass pub; for a pint of Pedigree, you'd go to a Marston's pub; etc. However, following the passage in 1989 of the *Beer Orders*, many formerly affiliated or *tied* pubs became *free houses*, permitted to carry beer from any brewer.

Off Sales and Off Sales Windows:
Many English pubs sell alcohol for consumption off the premises as well as on. Alcohol to be consumed off the premises is purchased from the *Off Sales Window* if there is one; otherwise it is bought over the bar. You may buy bottled beer or else provide the landlord with a container to be filled directly from the cask or pump.

Pub hours:
Restrictions demanded by the National Temperance Federation, and introduced during WWI, reduced pub drinking hours to 5½ hours/day (with a 2 hour break in the afternoon), and restricted closing hours to no later than 1 hour after sunset (and never later than 9pm). Sunday pub hours were limited to 4 (except for Wales where drinking in clubs and pubs on a Sunday was prohibited).[18] The passage in 1988 of the *Licensing Act* allowed pubs to remain open, Mondays through Saturdays, from 11am until 11pm, and lifted the requirement to close in mid-afternoon[19]. It also allowed landlords to extend their Sunday hours, so they could open as early as noon and close as late as 11pm, but a mid-afternoon closure on Sundays (from 3pm until 7pm) was still required. Since that time, the Sunday mid-afternoon closure requirement has been lifted;

---

[18]However, hours could vary depending upon the county, country, or specially granted dispensations (e.g., market day opening).

[19] Some pubs still opt to close from 3pm to 6pm so check before planning any country walks around pubs.

however, a number of pubs still do close mid-afternoon Sundays so it's best to check before stopping in.

There are pockets here and there where pub hours differ from the norm so when planning a trip to an unfamiliar area, it's best to check ahead.

Utility bills

In the US, utility companies bill customers monthly. In England customers are billed quarterly, unless otherwise requested. Utility bills may be paid by cheque, cash, direct debit, or with *Prepayment Stamps* purchased from a Post Office.

VAT

VAT (Value Added Tax) is currently 17.5%. Value added tax is *added to* all hotel and restaurant bills. However, it is already *incorporated into* the prices of most goods so the price marked on an item is the price you pay (unlike the US where sales tax is *added on* at the checkout counter). There is no local sales tax in cities and towns so if a single item is marked £3.99, then that is the price to pay.

MAIL ORDER AND SHOPPING GUIDE

The following is a brief list of shops that carry American foods and cooking ingredients -- a *complete* list would encompass another book so for listings of additional food shops, see the current edition of the *Food Lovers' Guide to Britain*, published by BBC Books.

Alma Delicatessen, 89 Lower Precinct, Coventry CV1 1DS
 Tel: 01203-228898

Essington Fruit Farm (*for picking your own fruit*)
 Bognop Road, Essington, Wolverhampton WV11 2BA
 Tel: 01902-735724
 (ring first to be sure the fruit you want is ready for picking)

Fortnum & Mason, 181 Piccadilly, London W1A 1ER
 Tel: 0171-734-8040

Harrods Ltd., Knightsbridge, London SW1X 7XL
 Tel: 0171-730-1234 Fax: 0171-581-0470

Note: *Jerry's Homestore specialise in furnishings rather than food but as they do carry some American foods, I've included their addresses. I would suggest though, first ringing ahead to see if what you need is something they carry.*
Jerry's Homestore, 163 Fulham Road, London SW3
 Tel: 0171-581-0909 Fax: 0171-584-3749

 57 Heath Street, Hampstead, NW3
 Tel: 0171-794-8622 Fax: 0171-794-8427

 Harvey Nichols, (concessions on 4th floor), Knightsbridge SW1
 Tel: 0171-245-6251 Fax: 245-1179

 The Bentall Centre, Kingston upon Thames, Surrey
 Tel: 0181-549-5393 Fax: 0181-549-9106

Lupe Pintos (*Mexican-American foods*), 24 Leven Street, Edinburgh,
 Tel: 0131-228-6241 Fax: 0131-228-2390

Note: *Made in America carry an exhaustive range of American foods which you can mail order.*
Made in America -- The American Store
Unit 5B, Hathaway Retail Park, Chippenham, Wilts. SN15 1JG
Tel: 01249-447558 Fax: 01249-446142

Partridges of Sloane Street, 132/134 Sloane Street, London SW1
Tel: 0171-730-0651 & 0171-730-7102/3 Fax: 0171-730-7104

Panzer Delicatessen
13-19 Circus Road, St John's Wood, London NW8 6PB
Tel: 0171-722-8596

Susman's Best Beef Biltong Co. (*Beef jerky & biltong - mail order*)
36 Hillcrest Rd., E. Sussex BN9 9EG
Tel: 01273-516160

James Trehane & Sons (*for blueberry picking*)
Stapehill Road, Hampreston, Wimborne, Dorset BH21 7ND
Tel: 01202-873490 (ring first to be sure fruit is ready for picking)

Note: *Trustins supply shops in England with international foods. To find the shop nearest you that carries a particular American product supplied by Trustin, write Trustin, enclosing a self-addressed, stamped envelope, and tell them exactly what you're looking for.*
Trustin the Foodfinders
Chase Rd., Northern Way, Bury St Edmunds, Suffolk IP32 6NT
Tel: 01284-766265

Note: *Walsh's manufacture an extract for making sarsaparilla beer and that's why they're included here -- they are not a shop.*
R. Walsh & Co. Ltd., 121 Rear Hamilton St., Blackburn, Lancashire

BIBLIOGRAPHY

American Heritage Cookbook American Heritage/Wings Books 1980

Bailey, A. (contributing editor) *Cook's Ingredients* Dorling Kindersley 1990

Beard, James *Beard on Bread* Alfred A Knopf 1993

_____ *The New James Beard* Alfred A Knopf 1981

Bissell, Frances *The Real Meat Cookbook* Chatto & Windus 1992

Blythman, Joanna *The Food We Eat* Michael Joseph 1996

Butler, Cleora *Cleora's Kitchens - The Memoir of a Cook* Council Oak Books, Ltd. 1985

CAMRA *Good Beer Guide 1998* CAMRA Books 1997/8

Complete Book of Chocolate Ebury Press (Good Housekeeping) 1993

Complete Guide to Food and Cooking Meredith Corporation (Better Homes and Gardens® Books) 1991

Cookery Year, The Reader's Digest 1973

CRC Handbook of Chemistry & Physics, 2nd edition, 1971-1972 Library of Congress 1971

Cunningham, Marion *The Fanny Farmer Cookbook* Alfred A Knopf 1994

Economist Measurement Guide & Reckoner Economist Newspaper 1975

Gelb, Barbara L. *Dictionary of Food and What's in It for You* Paddington Press 1978

Glover, Brian *Brewing for Victory* Lutterworth Press 1995

Green, Henrietta *Food Lovers' Guide to Britain 1996-1997* BBC Books 1995

Greer, Carlotta C. *School and Home Cooking* Allyn and Bacon 1925

Grigson, J. *The Observer Guide to European Cookery* Michael Joseph 1983

Grigson, S. *Ingredients Book* Pyramid Books 1991

Hadamuscin, John *Enchanted Evenings* Harmony Books 1990

Hadamuscin, John *Special Occasions* Harmony Books 1988

Herbst, Sharon Tyler *Food Lover's Companion* Barron's Educational Series, Inc. 1995

Hillman, Howard *Kitchen Science* Houghton Mifflin 1989

Jaffrey, Madhur *World of the East Vegetarian Cooking* Alfred A Knopf 1981

Katzen, Mollie *Moosewood Cookbook* Ten Speed Press 1977

Larousse Gastronomique Hamlyn 1988

Leith, Prue *The Cook's Handbook* Windward 1981

Lomask, Martha *The All-American Cookbook* Guild Publishing 1981

Mariani, John F. *The Dictionary of American Food and Drink* Hearst Books 1994

Medved, Eva *The World of Food* Ginn and Company 1973

Mendelsohn, Oscar A. *The Dictionary of Drink and Drinking* MacMillan 1965

Moosewood Collective *Sundays at Moosewood* Simon & Schuster/Fireside 1990

New Cookery Encyclopedia, The Leopard Books (Good Housekeeping) 1995

Protz, Roger *The Great British Beer Book* Impact Books 1993

Roden, Claudia *The Book of Jewish Food* Alfred A. Knopf 1997

Rombauer, I. and Becker, M. *Joy of Cooking* Bobbs-Merrill 1979

Sahni, Julie *Classic Indian Cooking* William Morrow & Co., Inc. 1980

Smith, Drew *Food Watch* HarperCollins 1994

Stanton, Rosemary *Complete Book of Food and Nutrition* Simon & Schuster Australia 1989

Stobart, Tom *The Cook's Encyclopaedia* Papermac 1982

Sunset Books *Fish & Shellfish* Lane Publ. Co. 1989

Tidy, Rosa *Rosa Tidy's Past Book* Lennard Publishers 1990

Widcombe, Richard *The Complete Book of Cheese* Summit Books 1978

Williams, Chuck *The Williams-Sonoma Cookbook and Guide to Kitchenware* Random House 1986

Yarwood, Doreen *The British Kitchen* B T Batsford Ltd 1981

ADDENDUM

Writing a book on what foods are currently available in a particular country is like trying to freeze time: you can't do it. Hence, this Addendum.

Re: Mirin
At the time I first wrote the mirin entry, it was not available in either of the 2 largest cities near me; as of this writing, it is. Still, should I find that when I actually need the mirin, I'm not able to get to one of these cities, there is an alternative. To substitute for one cup of mirin, combine ²/₃ cup (5¹/₃ oz.) dry sherry with ¹/₃ cup (2¹/₂ oz.) sugar (or alternatively, combine ³/₄ cup [6 oz.] dry sherry with ¹/₄ cup [2¹/₄ oz.] honey).

Re: Orange juice
When I began writing this book, cans of frozen concentrated juice were only available to the food trade -- not to the general public as in the US. However, by the time this book was ready for printing (mid-1998), I found Sainsburys had started selling frozen concentrated orange juice. The Sainsbury product is made in Israel from Jaffa oranges and comes in little 190g containers. I bought it on two separate occasions and unfortunately, both times found its flavour to be much more bitter than the reconstituted American product. Whether this was due to the different oranges used or to a difference in processing, I can't say, but it was sharp-tasting the way orange zest can be and, unless there's a change to its formula, I'd be surprised to see it catch on.
Incidentally, I neglected to mention when I first wrote the entry for orange juice, that you can also find it on your doorstep (provided you've asked your milkman to leave it).

Re: Sour cream
The sour cream produced in the US has usually been thickened through the addition of rennet extract, and most American recipes calling for sour cream were written with this thick sour cream in mind. To use British soured cream in American recipes, combine it first with

something thicker like *fromage frais* or, if you don't mind the extra calories, double or clotted cream. Alternatively, you could substitute for the sour cream altogether, using crème fraîche and/or half-fat crème fraîche. I have tried thickening the British soured cream at home, by first warming it and then adding *rennet liquid*, and in a few tests, dry milk solids as well. Unfortunately, none of my tests yielded a cream as thick as the American one (and often not noticeably thicker than the British one).

Re: Tomato puree
The 1990s saw a sharp increase in the variety of tomato-based sauces available in England and very recently, a product called *creamed tomatoes*, which is quite similar to American tomato puree, has appeared in Safeway stores. Whether the demand for *creamed tomatoes, passata, salsina*, et al. is enough to justify their continued availability is yet to be seen. So, if by the time you read this they are no longer available, you may substitute by blending approximately 3 medium skinned tomatoes for every cup of tomato puree called for.

INDEX

FEEDBACK AND QUESTIONS

Should sales merit a reprinting of *American Cooking in England*, I'm sure it will have to be a revised edition rather than a straight reprint as already, with this copy nearly at the printers, people are pointing out terms I've neglected to include. This is the danger of living in a foreign country -- you forget your native language: 'Oh, do we call it that in the States? I'd forgotten.' So, for those of you who haven't forgotten your American, and who have noticed either a term which should have been included but wasn't, or one which I've incorrectly described, please let me know.

Write to: Glencoe House Publications
              PO Box 5149
              Burton upon Trent
              Staffordshire
              DE14 3WZ

About the author:
Delora Jones is not a known cookery book writer; does not host a TV cookery show; nor does she earn her living as a caterer. She is simply an American who loves food and who, after moving to England in the early 1990s, found that cooking from American cookbooks here was an ordeal -- too many ingredients were either not available or called by different names. After searching for an American-to-English translation cookery book and finding none, she decided to research and write about the subject herself. Delora lives in Burton upon Trent with her husband, Roger Owen, and their two cats. She has also written a pocket-sized companion guide called *The Pocketbook Guide to American Cooking in England.*

How to Order Additional Copies

You may order additional copies of the main book; the pocketbook; or both together (at a savings).

To order:

- write to the address below, stating the number of copies required, and of which book(s);

- enclose a cheque made out to *Glencoe House Publications* to cover the cost of the copies, and their postage and packaging. Allow 28 days for delivery.

To order the main book:	To order the pocketbook:	To order both books:	
American Cooking in England	*The Pocketbook Guide to American Cooking in England*	*American Cooking in England*	*The Pocketbook Guide to American Cooking in England*
book: £14.99	book: £3.99	both books: £17.99	
p&p: 2.75	p&p: .30	p&p: 2.75	
total: **£17.74**	total: **£4.29**	total: **£20.74**	

Send your order and cheque to:

Glencoe House Publications
PO Box 5149
Burton upon Trent
Staffordshire
DE14 3WZ